Palestine in Crisis

The Struggle for Peace and
Political Independence after Oslo

Graham Usher

Pluto Press
LONDON • EAST HAVEN, CT
in association with
Transnational Institute (TNI) and
Middle East Research & Information Project (MERIP)

First published 1995 by Pluto Press
345 Archway Road, London N6 5AA
and 140 Commerce Street,
East Haven, CT 06512, USA
in association with
the Transnational Institute (TNI),
Paulus Potterstraat 20, 1071 DA, Amsterdam

British Library Cataloguing in Publication Data
A catalogue record for this book is available from the British Library

ISBN 0 7453 0969 0 hbk

Library of Congress Cataloging-in-Publication Data
A catalog record for this book is available from the Library of Congress

Designed and produced for Pluto Press by
Chase Production Services, Chipping Norton, OX7 5QR
Typeset from disk by Stanford Desktop Publishing Services
Printed in the EC by T J Press, Padstow, England

Contents

Acknowledgements

All journalism is the result of a collaborative effort, but this book really couldn't have happened without the support of the following people and institutions.

First of all, my various editors who, for the last year or so, have allowed me to earn my living as a journalist, especially: Michael Wall and Steve Sherman at *Middle East International*, Barbara Smith at *The Economist*, Paul Anderson at *New Statesman/Society*, Micah Sifry and JoAnn Wypijewski at *The Nation*, Denise Searle and Joe Hanlon at *Red Pepper*, Hein Marais at Work in Progress and (now) South African Broadcasting, and to all at the Institute of Race Relations (*Race & Class*) who taught me, way back, that 'the people we are fighting for should be the people we are writing for'.

Second, my various Palestinian, Israeli and other friends who, at one time or another, have given over to me their time, patience and intellect, especially: Haider Abd al-Shafi, Saleh Abd al-Shafi, Achmed Abdallah, Eqbal Ahmad, Talal Aukal, Haim Baram, Hassan Barghouti, Marwan Barghouti, Yizhar Be'er, Fuad Fargawi, Ismail Fargawi, Rita Giacamen, Amira Hass, Jamil Hilal, Islah Jad, Bassem Jarrar, Saleh Abdel Jawad, Ghazi Abu Jiab, Bassam Joudeh, Marwan Ali Kafarna, Nasser Ali Kafarna, Qassem Ali Kafarna, Umayya Khammash, Iatimad Mohanna, Amna Rimayeh, Mahmoud Shaban, Israel Shahak, Khalil Shahin, Adnan Abu Shami, Taher Shriteh, Raji Sourani, Ron Wilkinson, Sufian Abu Zaida and Jamal Zaqqout.

Third, to those who took time out to read the drafts and comment on the drift and shape of my argument. Their criticisms were always taken on board, if not always accepted, especially: Lamis Andoni, Rema Hammami, Alex Pollock, Salim Tamari and Maja van der Velden.

I want to give a special thanks to MERIP editor Joe Stork, and everyone at MERIP, including assistant editor Maggy Zanger, Lisa Hajjar, and interns Peter Ogram and Leena Khan. Thanks also to Pluto and the Transnational Institute who collectively nurtured the text into a book, and to the Foundation for Middle East Peace for the accompanying maps.

Finally, to Mark Taylor – friend, flatmate and (for his sins) accused pseudonym. I doubt if there is a single word here that has not been bounced off him first. If there is to be a dedication, it is to him.

Needless to say – and to the immense relief of all of the above – the conclusions drawn from this study of the post-Oslo Palestinian experience are entirely my own.

Foreword

In the preamble to the Declaration of Principles signed on 13 September 1993, Israel and the Palestine Liberation Organisation 'agree[d] that it is time to put an end to decades of confrontation and conflict'. It was immediately apparent that the documents negotiated secretly in Oslo had changed the environment and the parameters of that conflict. But as we approach the second anniversary of that carefully choreographed first handshake of Yitzhak Rabin and Yasir Arafat on the White House lawn, it is equally clear that a fairly-negotiated just peace and comprehensive reconciliation is not at hand.

In October 1993, a few weeks after the much-hyped handshake, Jochen Hippler and Mariano Aguirre of the Transnational Institute (TNI) approached me to write a short critical account of the circumstances that produced the Oslo Accords and the implications for the Palestinian-Israeli conflict. I agreed with their assessment that such a project was important. There was a need to query and challenge the self-serving consensus of the political elites and media – American, European, Israeli and also now Arab governments and the PLO – that the conflict had been consigned to history. Groups and individuals in Europe and North America who had aligned themselves in solidarity with Palestinian and Israeli peace forces were looking for analysis and perspective that avoided both the euphoric self-congratulations of the various governments and their media on the one hand, and the reflexive condemnation of some Palestinian opposition groups on the other.

I expressed my view that the author should not be someone following developments from North America or Europe but rather someone close to the ground, as it were, someone deeply familiar with the situation in Gaza and the West Bank, yet detached from Palestinian factional politics. I suggested that the Middle East Research and Information Project (MERIP) be given a contract to produce such a text, and TNI agreed.

Graham Usher was our first choice for this assignment. He had been living in Gaza for a number of years and had done several excellent interviews for Middle East Report. We had long admired his biweekly reports from Gaza and the West Bank for the London-based *Middle East International*. Graham agreed to accept the assignment and the result is this book.

Usher provides here the best available account we have seen of the conditions and circumstances in the West Bank and Gaza, and in the PLO, leading up to the Declaration of Principles. The main strength of his text, though, is his fully integrated analysis of the different dimensions – political, socioeconomic and cultural – of the Palestinian experience in the post-Oslo period. He discusses key sectors of Palestinian political society, including the working classes, the women's movement and the Islamists. Much of his account draws on his unparalleled access to activists and militants from across the Palestinian political spectrum, from Hamas and the secular opposition to representatives of Arafat's Fatah organisation. Usher's treatment of Hamas and the phenomenon of political Islam in Palestinian politics, in particular, will usefully offset the simplistic reporting and commentary and the political misreadings that prevail in the West on this topic.[1]

The result is a convincing, and profoundly disquieting, articulation of the political character of the Palestinian Authority that has emerged under Arafat's direction. This book thus addresses an important and complicated aspect of a long-standing confrontation that, despite all grand pronouncements to the contrary, is still very much alive. Other aspects – Israeli political and socioeconomic circumstances, for instance, and the impact of the post-Oslo negotiations on Israeli electoral dynamics – deserve a comparably detailed, nuanced and engaged treatment. At another level, whatever its effect on the Israeli-Palestinian conflict, Oslo has almost certainly spelt the end of the broader confrontation between Israel and the Arab states, and an analysis of the regional dynamics surrounding Oslo is sorely needed.

This book necessarily addresses a particular moment, namely, the period leading up to and following the Declaration of Principles. That agreement resolved certain long-standing contradictions, but at the price of creating new ones and making more acute many that remain. The key issues in the conflict – land and water rights, Jerusalem, Israeli settlements, Palestinian rights of return – will be negotiated, perhaps, only after September 1996. In any event, the dynamic of occupation and resistance continues, transformed but not replaced by anything that remotely can be termed 'peace'.[2]

Finally, the events and dynamics that Usher persuasively analyses here have unfolded against a backdrop of unstinting US government support for Israeli intransigence, and for the most authoritarian aspects of Arafat's rule, such as the establishment of so-called state security courts, complete with secret trials, and mass arrests directed exclusively at Palestinian political opponents of Oslo.

The term 'peace process', after Oslo as before, is a mantra invoked by those in power to refer exclusively to terms of American-Israeli imposition. This 'peace process' today is, by all accounts, in deep trouble. The spin-meisters of Washington and Tel Aviv attribute this trouble to 'the enemies of peace', a roster presently headed by Iran, Hamas and the Lebanese Islamist party Hizaballah, 'Islamic terrorists' all.[3]

In fact, as Usher's text demonstrates, this trouble derives from readily observable facts of life on the ground. One is the increasing pauperisation of much of the Palestinian population, especially in Gaza. Another is the accelerated confiscation of Palestinian land by the Israeli army, both for settlement expansion and for some 15 new highways that will connect the settlements with Israel proper, and with each other, bypassing and in effect segmenting Palestinian towns and villages into isolated cantons and facilitating Israeli military control from the 'outside'.[4]

A third is the closure of all of occupied East Jerusalem for much of the two years since the signing of the Declaration of Principles. Jerusalem's significance is not only, or even primarily, symbolic or religious. 'Greater Jerusalem' comprises the 2.5 square miles of the city that had been under Jordanian occupation and a further 24.5 square miles of annexed West Bank lands.[5] Its administrative, economic and social, as well as political and communications, functions have been put off-limits to most Palestinians. The closure also has effectively divided the residents of the northern and southern parts of the West Bank from each other. Workers, proprietors and professionals cannot reach their shops and offices; patients cannot see their doctors. These are some of the everyday implications of Israel's defining of Jerusalem, with US support, as separate and non-negotiable.

With Oslo and particularly with the subsequent Cairo Accord of May 1994, the 'peace process' has shifted to some extent, with the important exception of Jerusalem, from an imposition of occupation to an imposition of separation – not in the form of two states, Israeli and Palestinian, but in a manner resembling that of South Africa's structuring of apartheid.[6] What all this may mean for the future of the Israeli-Palestinian confrontation is difficult say. The negative features of this transformation have become quite apparent in the two years since Arafat and Rabin met on the White House lawn. In the longer term, this revised dynamic of oppression may unlock new political forces and leaderships among both Palestinians and Israelis. One indication of this can be seen in the strategic debates of Palestinian Islamists. The Palestinian leadership furthermore includes in its cadre articulate exponents of a democratic society based on the rule of law.[7] In the view of Palestinian political philosopher and activist Azmy Bishara, a critic of the PLO, 'the new political conditions formed in the wake of the Oslo Accords' dictate a programme of political resistance oriented not towards an independent Palestinian state but bi-nationalism, endorsing civic and political equality and rejecting separation.[8] The May 1995 role of the Palestinian Israeli members of parliament in forcing the Rabin government to suspend its confiscation of some 134 acres in East Jerusalem for settler housing may come to be seen as a harbinger of such a bi-national strategy.

The future of the Palestinian struggle for political rights remains uncertain. How that struggle has come to its present dilemma is the subject of Graham Usher's excellent book.

Joe Stork
July 1995

Joe Stork is a co-founder of the Middle East Research and Information Project (MERIP) and editor of its bi-monthly magazine, *Middle East Report*.

Mediterranean Sea

Jenin

West Bank
(Israeli occupied —
status to be determined)

Tulkarem

Nablus

Qalqilia

Tel Aviv

Ariel

Ma'ale Ephraim

ISRAEL

Ramallah

Givat Ze'ev

Jericho

Jerusalem

Ma'ale Adumim

Bethlehem

Etzion Bloc

Efrat

Hebron

Kiryat Arba

Dead

Sea

Jordan River

——— 1949 Armistice Line

- - - - 1967 Cease-fire Line

◼ Lands under Israeli control

▲ Israeli settlement

● Palestinian City

▮ Annexed East Jerusalem

0   5   10 Miles

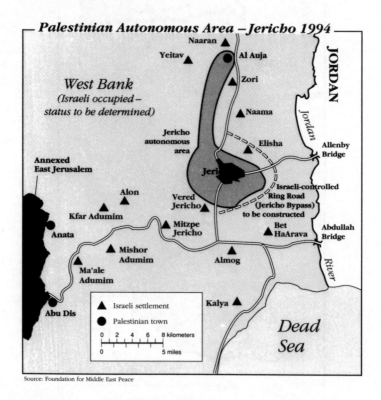

Palestinian Autonomous Area – Jericho 1994

Naaran

Yeitav

Al Auja

Zori

West Bank
*(Israeli occupied –
status to be determined)*

Naama

Jericho
autonomous
area

Elisha

Allenby
Bridge

JORDAN

Jordan

**Annexed
East Jerusalem**

Jeri

Alon

Vered
Jericho

Israeli-controlled
Ring Road
(Jericho Bypass)
to be constructed

Kfar Adumim

Anata

Mitzpe
Jericho

Bet
HaArava

Abdullah
Bridge

Mishor
Adumim

Almog

River

Ma'ale
Adumim

▲ Israeli settlement

● Palestinian town

Kalya

Abu Dis

0 2 4 6 8 kilometers

0   5 miles

**Dead
Sea**

Source: Foundation for Middle East Peace

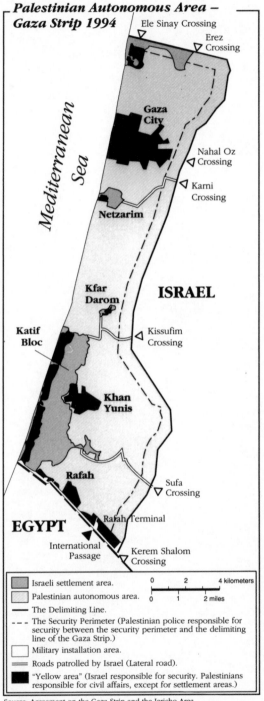

Palestinian Autonomous Area – Gaza Strip 1994

Ele Sinay Crossing

Erez Crossing

Mediterranean Sea

Gaza City

Nahal Oz Crossing

Karni Crossing

Netzarim

Kfar Darom

ISRAEL

Katif Bloc

Kissufim Crossing

Khan Yunis

Rafah

Sufa Crossing

EGYPT

Rafah Terminal

International Passage

Kerem Shalom Crossing

	Israeli settlement area.
	Palestinian autonomous area.
——	The Delimiting Line.
- - -	The Security Perimeter (Palestinian police responsible for security between the security perimeter and the delimiting line of the Gaza Strip.)
	Military installation area.
===	Roads patrolled by Israel (Lateral road).
	"Yellow area" (Israel responsible for security. Palestinians responsible for civil affairs, except for settlement areas.)

0   2   4 kilometers

0   1   2 miles

Source: Agreement on the Gaza Strip and the Jericho Area.

1

Behind the Oslo Agreement

In the PLO's letter of 'mutual recognition' to the Israeli government signed on 9 September 1993 – one of the four documents that constitute the Oslo accords – PLO Chairman, Yasir Arafat, expressed his 'firm conviction' that the 'PLO considers the signing of the Declaration of Principles (DOP) ... a historic event, inaugurating a new epoch of peaceful coexistence, free from violence and all other acts which endanger peace and stability'.[1] On 13 September, Arafat duly shook Yitzak Rabin's hand and signed the Declaration on the White House lawn.

Nine months later, Arafat returned to Palestine, ready to install his fledgeling Palestinian National Authority (PNA) first in the 'autonomous enclaves' of Gaza and Jericho and subsequently throughout the West Bank. On 2 July, he addressed a rally in Gaza's Jabalya refugee camp. With more than 70,000 Palestinian refugees crammed into a living area of 1.5 square kilometres, Jabalya is the largest refugee camp in the occupied territories and an enduring emblem of Israel's 27-year military rule. Jabalya was also the birthplace of the intifada, the mass Palestinian revolt against Israel's rule that erupted in December 1987. 'I know many of you here think Oslo is a bad agreement', Arafat said to a packed schoolyard. 'It is a bad agreement. But it's the best we can get in the worst situation.'

What accounts for the fall from the optimism redolent in Arafat's first declaration to the pessimism conceded in the second? The answer lies in the comprehension of the 'worst situation' to which Arafat referred. This 'worst situation' was not only the precondition for the Oslo accords but also their political significance.

At the time of the Washington ceremony, the PLO was gripped by the worst crisis of its 29-year history. Regionally, Arafat's decision to stand by Baghdad in the wake of the second Gulf war of 1990–91 estranged the PLO from Egypt and the Arab states of the Persian Gulf, and cost the organisation $120 million in annual donations from Saudi Arabia, Kuwait and Iraq. Confiscations of Palestinian deposits in Kuwaiti banks, plus the loss of other revenues, brought PLO forfeits from the Gulf states in the years 1991–93 to around $10 billion.[2]

Internationally, the collapse of the socialist bloc in Eastern Europe, and of the Soviet Union in particular, removed what for the PLO had been a historic counterweight to the imperial and pro-Israeli designs of the United States in the region. The Soviet collapse also prompted massive Soviet Jewish emigration to Israel with 390,682 settling there and in the territories in the years 1990–92.[3]

These factors were compounded by the PLO's rapidly diminish- ing manoeuvring room in its previous spheres of influence. Lebanon had already imposed draconian restrictions on its Palestinian residents. This was aggravated by a Syrian-sponsored siege waged by the Amal movement against Palestinian refugee camps in the late 1980s. In August 1990, the Gulf countries, as punishment for Arafat's solidarity with Saddam Hussein, summarily expelled nearly 400,000 Pales- tinians who worked there. There was no possibility of any PLO mobilisation in Syria given the frigid relations between Arafat and Asad. Finally, relations between the PLO and its constituency in Jordan – the largest concentration of Palestinians outside the West Bank and Gaza – were increasingly tense. King Hussein was histori- cally suspicious of any PLO activity on his turf and his 1988 decision to renounce all claims to the West Bank had worked to strain Pales- tinian allegiances.

All of this dramatically affected the PLO, in both the occupied ter- ritories and the diaspora. The cut-off of Gulf state funds triggered a dynamic of disintegration throughout the organisation. Thousands of functionaries were laid off, missions abroad closed and, crucially, educational, welfare and social services for Palestinian refugees suspended. In August 1993, the very eve of Oslo, the PLO in Tunis simply closed down the organisation's information, culture, social affairs and 'returnee' departments for want of funds.

Madrid

The only thing the PLO had going for it in the period before Oslo was the 'peace process' that followed from the Madrid Conference of October 1991. Madrid was the fruit of then-US President George Bush's new dispensation for the region, part of the 'new world order' he proclaimed after the fall of communism. The ostensible reason behind Bush's call was to end 'the painful and intractable ... dispute between Israel and its neighbours', but the real imperative driving it was somewhat different.[4] The Gulf war had thrown together a coalition of Arab states more susceptible to US hegemony than at any point in the last 40 years. With the collapse of the Soviet Union, and the defeat of Saddam's degenerate but independent brand of Arab nationalism, Egypt, Syria and the Arabian Peninsula countries needed to shore up their authoritarian and discredited regimes with some gesture of US concern for Arab grievances.

These grievances focused on Israel's ongoing occupation of Gaza, the West Bank, Jerusalem, the Golan Heights and South Lebanon. No Arab leader could dare endorse a post-Gulf war settlement that left blatantly unresolved the question of the Palestinians. Bush's Gulf war victory statement before the US Congress on 6 March 1991 therefore referred to the need for a 'comprehensive peace [which] must be grounded in United Nations Security Council Resolutions 242 and 338 and the principle of territory for peace'. This rhetorical accommodation to those Arab states that had backed the anti-Saddam alliance also appeared to mark the possibility of the PLO's international rehabilitation after the catastrophe of the war.

This position on Washington's part, coupled with the Bush administration's letter of assurances to the Palestinian side in October 1991 committing the administration to 'oppose settlement activity in the territories occupied in 1967', enabled Arafat to marshal a PLO Executive Committee majority in favour of the 'Madrid formula'. But the concessions the PLO was forced to make simply to sit down at the table with the Israelis were to leave their imprint on Oslo.

To begin with, the PLO had to give up any formal role in the peace process. In its stead was a delegation of Palestinians from the territories, excluding Jerusalem, approved by the Shamir government and functioning ostensibly as part of a combined delegation with Jordan. The bilateral format of the negotiations – with the Israelis holding separate talks with Lebanon, Syria and Palestine/Jordan – also allowed Israel to play off one against the other.

There were ten laboured rounds of negotiations between 1991 and 1993. The bases of these post-Madrid negotiations rent the delicate PLO unity so carefully stitched together after the October 1988 Palestinian National Council (PNC) meeting in Algiers, where the movement had formally opted for a two-state solution to the Palestinian/Israeli conflict. Israeli negotiators continually focused on the specifics of Palestinian self-government – such as the nature of an 'autonomous' authority, its structure and legislative power – while avoiding any discussion of substantive issues such as the applicability of UN Security Council Resolution 242 to the process or the idea of transition from the 'interim period of Palestinian self-government' to a final status settlement.[5]

Many Palestinians, including those initially supportive of Madrid, began to view Israel's stonewalling as a cover for escalating land confiscation and military repression in the territories. In 1991, the year of Madrid, Israel expropriated a further 187,000 dunums (46,750 acres) of Palestinian land in the West Bank and Gaza, and established eight settlements comprising 13,650 new housing units. The confiscations marked a threefold increase over 1990 levels, while the number of settlement starts was 60 per cent greater than the average for all the years between 1967 and 1990. This was *de facto* annexation, and it was no longer creeping: it was raging.[6]

If Palestinian hopes were revived slightly by the Israeli election in June 1992 of a Labour government pledged 'to make peace with the Palestinians within nine months', they were quickly dashed when Rabin's negotiators signalled that they planned to take up where Shamir's had left off. Even Rabin's much vaunted 'settlement freeze', made in exchange for Bush's release to Israel of $10 billion in 'loan guarantees', was hedged by the exclusion of 24,000 units under construction in East Jerusalem and the territories and by the proviso that an annual increase of 1000–2000 units in the West Bank would be allowed to account for 'natural growth'.[7]

The Occupied Territories

Madrid also coincided with, and to some extent accelerated, a degeneration of the uprising in the occupied territories. The formation of a Palestinian 'Madrid' delegation consecrated a process in which leadership of the intifada shifted decisively from the territories to the PLO in Tunis.[8] The delegation was from the West Bank and Gaza, but it was wholly controlled by Arafat. 'I have a letter in my pocket from the PLO authorising me to be here', said Palestinian delegate Saeb Erekat during his first meeting with US Secretary of State James Baker, 'and without it this meeting could not take place. That is the reality everyone has to be aware of.'[9]

Such control was then taken as a symbolic victory of sorts, demonstrating Arafat's ability to go beyond the text of Madrid and render absurd Shamir's claim that in talking to Palestinian delegates he was not talking to the PLO. Such diplomatic scores, however, were not complemented by any PLO policy on the ground. Without a political strategy that addressed the situation in territories as much as it exploited the diplomatic opportunities offered by Madrid, the PLO's 'last card' – the mobilising potential of Palestinians under occupation – was liable to be undermined.

In the wake of the PLO's 1982 military defeat in Lebanon, the occupied territories had become the principal site of the national struggle. The 1987–88 outbreak of the uprising and especially the emergence of the Unified National Leadership (UNL), a body comprised of local PLO factions but nevertheless relatively independent from Tunis, was the subjective expression of this reality.[10] By the early 1990s, though, the intifada was in deep internal crisis. Under the stewardship of Likud Defence Minister Moshe Arens, the Israeli army had moved away from the high profile confrontational 'force, might and beatings' approach, a hallmark of its predecessor Yitzak Rabin. Instead, the Israeli's targeted more selective and covert operations against 'intifada activists', relying on greater use of undercover units and the recuperation of intelligence networks based on Palestinian collaborators.[11]

The upshot was a security offensive that succeeded in divesting the uprising of its mass character, turning it instead into the private property of rival bands of armed 'strike forces'. Initially the uprising had embodied a unifying strategy mobilising Palestinians around concrete and achievable goals.[12] By 1991 it had deteriorated into a domestic affair, with an increase in collaborator killings and, on occasion, outbreaks of factional violence. The inter-PLO dissensions thrown up by Madrid, with the PLO's Popular and Democratic Fronts (PFLP and DFLP) coming down firmly against the Conference, aggravated the drift to internecine struggle.

To add to its woes, the PLO confronted for the first time in the territories an indigenous, authentic and mass opposition completely outside of its sway – the Islamic Resistance Movement, known by its Arab acronym, Hamas. Formed in 1988 as the 'intifada wing' of the Muslim Brothers in Palestine, by the early 1990s Hamas had grown through a subtle mix of largely social and culturalist tactics into the most significant political force in the territories after the UNL. The Islamists rejected Madrid, aggressively challenging the PLO's claim of sole representative of the Palestinian people. In late 1991, in open defiance of the UNL, Hamas mounted a series of ominously well-supported strikes against the 'peace process'. (In July 1992, street battles between Hamas and Fatah supporters erupted in Gaza, leaving 100 injured and three dead.)[13]

This domestic heat increased with the election of Rabin, whose 'peace plan' Hamas viewed with trepidation as undercutting the rejectionist basis of its support. Hamas's response proved spectacular and far-reaching.

In December 1992, Hamas guerrillas killed six Israeli soldiers in as many days, including the kidnap and assassination of Israeli Border police officer, Nissim Toledano. Hamas asserted this was in retaliation for the life sentence Israel had meted out to the movement's spiritual leader, Sheikh Ahmad Yassin.

The Rabin government, in response, rounded up some 1600 Palestinians suspected of Hamas connections and summarily expelled 415 of them to southern Lebanon. These actions immediately scuttled the post-Madrid negotiations in Washington, and pitched the territories into their worst period of violence since the intifada – and arguably since the occupation began in 1967. In March 1993 alone, 28 Palestinians and 15 Israelis were killed; most of the Israelis were slain inside Israel. Rabin 'indefinitely' closed off the territories, depriving 189,000 Palestinians of work.[14] This was among other 'tough new measures' designed to 'take Gaza out of Tel Aviv'.

During the spring of 1993, IDF patrols trawled through the territories with the express intent of 'reclaiming the towns and camps from masked gunmen'. 'Search operations' blew up scores of houses on the hunch that 'terrorists' might (or might not) reside in them. Undercover squads infiltrated camps and villages to flush out, and usually execute, 'masked youths'. Gaza, being the 'base of Hamas', bore the brunt of the punishment. Observation posts were set up with new 'open fire regulations'. 'If you see someone holding a cinderblock, Molotov cocktail or iron bar', announced an Israeli Border Police officer, 'you shoot him without making any bones about the matter. There is no longer a procedure for apprehending a suspect.'[15]

Dossiers compiled by Palestinian, Israeli and international human rights organisations testified to the human cost of this brutal new turn in Israel's counterinsurgency operations. Between February and May 1993, the IDF killed 67 Palestinians in the Gaza Strip alone, including 29 in May, making it the bloodiest month of the uprising. A staggering 1522 were wounded, 98 per cent of them from live ammunition. Ten 'search operations' left 450 people homeless or, as one Gazan put it, 'refugees from refugee camps'. Property damage amounted to about $50 million. Palestinians were beaten, their homes raided, their communities curfewed. Most human rights researchers simply gave up counting. By the time of Oslo, there were 17,000 Palestinians in Israeli jails, most of them rounded up in the preceding nine months.[16]

The military oppression wrought – and obscured – by the closure was also intended to compel the Palestinians to come round to Israel's way of thinking at the negotiations. Human rights violations, extrajudicial executions, the enduring illegality and violence of occupation – these were so many bargaining chips. 'You [the Palestinian delegation] want to solve the problem?', asked Rabin in April 1993. 'The place to do that is around the negotiating table. So it is permissible for me to keep the territories closed as long as possible.'[17]

The delegation – representing a people bloodied, exhausted and bereft of any political alternative – could do no other than submit and return to the negotiations, though they were aware that the Madrid formula was at an impasse. What none of them knew at the time, though Rabin did, was that the real import of the army's onslaught in Gaza was to determine the conditions of its withdrawal.

Secret Channel

While terror raged in Gaza, 'peace' was being negotiated, quietly, in hotels and country houses in Norway. This was the Oslo channel, a series of 14 secret meetings between PLO officials and Israeli government advisers and academics begun in late January 1993 and stretching over the next eight months, hosted and facilitated by Norway's Foreign Affairs Minister Johan Jorgen Holst and social scientist Terje Rod Larsen. Out of these meetings the Oslo accords were born.

Two events facilitated the Oslo channel. On 19 January 1993, the Knesset lifted the ban on Israeli contacts with the PLO. At the time observers regarded this as a gesture by Rabin to lure the Palestinian delegation back to the negotiating table. Shortly before that, though, the PLO's treasurer, Ahmad Qrei (Abu Ala), had circulated a discussion paper which argued that economic integration between the occupied territories and Israel should be the underpinning of any peace agreement between Israel and the Palestinians. The paper met with the approval of Israel's Deputy Foreign Minister Yossi Beilin, who had long believed that peace was conditional on Israel's recognising the PLO. In December 1992, he dispatched an Israeli academic, Yair Hirschfield, to London to meet 'illegally' with Qrei.[18]

Once the ban on PLO contacts was lifted – the next day in fact – talks began in earnest in Oslo. Hirschfield was joined on the Israeli side by a fellow don, Ron Pundak, and Qrei was supervised by Arafat's main political adviser, Mahmoud Abbas (Abu Mazen). By March 1993, with still no movement on the Madrid track and the territories teetering on the brink of anti-colonial war, Israeli Foreign Minister Shimon Peres upgraded the 'secret channel' by sending his deputy, Uri Savir, and legal adviser, Joel Singer. With their input, what had started as a discussion on future Israeli/Palestinian economic cooperation evolved rapidly into talks on a joint Declaration of Principles.

In substance, the Declaration's proposals for a Palestinian Autonomy Council largely rehashed that part of the Camp David accords signed between Menachem Begin and Anwar Sadat in 1978. The notion of early transfer of 'limited authority' to Palestinians in the West Bank and Gaza was lifted from Israeli position papers presented to the Madrid talks and repeatedly rebuffed by the Palestinian delegation, on Arafat's order. Arafat accused Israel of wanting to reduce the territories to 'bantustans' and Palestinians to the same status as 'North America's Indians'.

What was new in the Declaration was the procedure for Palestinian autonomy, especially Israel's pledge to withdraw militarily from the Gaza Strip and the West Bank town of Jericho as the 'first step'. This innovation bore the signature of Shimon Peres.

In the winter of 1993, the Israeli media and public were clamouring for Israel to decant 'unilaterally' from the 'hellhole' of Gaza. This outcry was predicated on a bizarre logic: since Hamas guerrillas were killing Jews, and Hamas was strong in Gaza, 'separation' from Gaza would mean a separation from 'terror'. Few Israelis had any kind of ideological attachment to Gaza, unlike areas of the West Bank and Jerusalem. Even Rabin, in an unguarded moment in December 1992, mused before an American Jewish delegation that he wished Gaza would 'disengage itself' from Israel and then 'sink' into the Mediterranean.

Peres figured that an Israeli withdrawal from Gaza would not only enjoy massive popularity on the Israeli street; it would also break the bottleneck of Bush's 'comprehensive' Madrid formula. Mahmoud Abbas took the idea to Arafat, who rejected it, but not outright. Were the withdrawal from Gaza to include the West Bank's Jericho as a way of signifying the 'integrity of the occupied territories', he suggested, there would be grounds for a deal. In August 1993, after some hesitation, Rabin agreed.

The Negotiating Agenda

The Declaration is not a peace treaty but an agenda for negotiations, covering a five-year 'interim period' which would then lead to a permanent settlement based on UN Security Council Resolutions 242 and 338. Its main provisions are as follows:

- Within two months of the DOP's 'coming into force', the IDF would commence withdrawal from Gaza and Jericho to be replaced by 'a strong Palestinian police force' responsible for Palestinian 'internal security and public order'.
- Israel would retain control of external relations and foreign affairs.
- Once the IDF's withdrawal from the two 'autonomous areas' was complete, the Israeli government would transfer to 'authorised

Palestinians' civil power over five services: education and culture, health, social welfare, direct taxation and tourism.

- Within nine months of withdrawal, Palestinians in the West Bank and Gaza would hold elections for a Palestinian Council which would assume responsibility for these five powers, plus others 'to be negotiated', but not defence or foreign affairs.
- 'No later than two years' after this, Israel and the Palestinians would start negotiations on a permanent settlement and address such issues as Jerusalem, settlements and the 1948 refugees.

The great attraction of the Declaration for the Israelis was its temporal spacing of the issues. 'While the proposal lacks the clarity of a map', said Peres, 'it provides the commitment of a calendar'.[19]

'The clarity of a map', however, was what most Palestinians had insisted the peace process was all about. The core of their conflict with Israel had always been land, specifically (and, after the Palestinian National Council of 1988, officially) the territories occupied in 1967. Yet it was on the issue of territoriality that the DOP was so deeply ambiguous.

The ambiguity sparked the domestic Palestinian debate that arose around the DOP. While the PLO's Marxist Popular and Democratic Fronts and the Islamist Hamas and Islamic Jihad denounced Oslo as 'Camp David in drag', others – including sections of Arafat's Fatah movement, the Palestinian People's (formerly Communist) Party (PPP), and the new Fida party (which had split from the Democratic Front) – were enthusiastic or non-committal.

For Hanan Ashrawi, the Palestinian delegation spokesperson, the merit of the DOP was its 'specification of 242'. This 'means that you recognise that [Jerusalem, the West Bank and Gaza] are occupied territory, that international law prevails and that withdrawal is a basic component of the agreement'. The DOP also appeared to offer 'certain key political concessions that we couldn't get in the [Madrid] negotiations', she said.[20] These were its commitment to continue Rabin's 'freeze' on land confiscation and the building of new settlements in the occupied territories (except Jerusalem); its transfer of 'five major portfolios' to a Palestinian authority whose jurisdiction would cover the West Bank as well as the autonomous regions of Gaza and Jericho; and its pledge to address in the interim phase the return of Palestinians 'displaced' in 1967.[21]

Among pro-Oslo Palestinians, perhaps the deciding factor in favour was that the Declaration's very ambiguities could be exploited to further Palestinians' national goals. 'Gaza–Jericho will not automatically lead to national independence', said Fatah leader, Marwan

Barghouti, 'but the political space it opens up enables us to set off an irreversible dynamic [towards independence] through the new national mechanisms we set in place'.[22]

For critics, the ambiguities remained the problem. For Haidar Abd al-Shafi, head of the Palestinian delegation, the DOP's gravest flaw was that it failed 'to address Israel's illegal claim to the occupied territories'. If the territories were not 'occupied', then they must be 'disputed' – the contention of every Israeli government since 1967. Abd al-Shafi argued that the notion of 'disputed' rather than 'occupied' territory pervaded every aspect of the DOP. Even where Palestinians are granted limited jurisdiction – over the 'five powers', for instance – this refers to 'Palestinians in the territories' but not the territories themselves. Israel's vaunted 'military withdrawal' from Palestinian population centres is hedged on the condition that, for the duration of the interim period, Israel would preserve jurisdiction over existing Israeli settlements and military installations, the so-called 'state lands' Israel had requisitioned since 1967 for 'security purposes'. At the time of Oslo, these lands comprised 65 per cent of the West Bank and 42 per cent of Gaza. 'Withdrawal', in other words, meant redeployment.

In the opinion of Abd al-Shafi, this augured 'a kind of apartheid'. Palestinian 'tacit acceptance of two separate entities in the Palestinian territories – two separate administrations, two separate judicial systems', he said, means 'we are conceding something that has been illegally established ... we have helped confer legitimacy on what Israel has established illegally'.[23]

Recognition

While the debate 'inside' was about the textual detail of the Declaration, the imperative driving Arafat and Abbas toward its endorsement hinged on a concession that does not even appear in the text: Israel's recognition of the PLO. On 8 August 1993, one hour before they were due to meet US Secretary of State Warren Christopher, the Palestinian delegation in Washington received faxed instructions and a document from Arafat in Tunis that they should submit as 'new bases' for negotiations. This document, essentially, was the Declaration. Mindful of their constituencies at home, the delegation was alarmed by its content. It overhauled positions they had previously been told to defend 'at all costs'. They were also angered by the cavalier way in which Arafat had relegated their status to that of a 'fax machine for Tunis'.

Delegation members Faisal Husseini, Hanan Ashrawi and Saeb Erekat tendered their resignations, demanding greater consultation with the 'leadership outside'. Arafat swiftly recalled them to Tunis and, amid much apologetics and shows of unity, 'upgraded' their status as fully-fledged members of a new PLO 'higher committee' responsible for 'directing the Palestinian peace delegation'.[23] Even at the time, this all smacked more of theatre than of substantive conflict. The meaning was clear: Israel was negotiating directly with Tunis. Two weeks later, Rabin conceded for the first time that 'there would be no escape from recognising the PLO'.[25]

It was not just the demise of the delegation that pushed Rabin toward recognition. First, he had flirted in July with a 'Syria first' option – the idea that Israel could cut a peace agreement with Syria before dealing with the Palestinians. This came to an abrupt halt when Asad signalled that while 'total peace' with Syria was on the table, the price would be Israel's 'total withdrawal' from the Golan Heights and the dismantling of settlements there. Second, 'internal security assessments' assured Rabin that Arafat's domestic and international plight was now so dire that, for the carrot of recognition, he would be amenable to making unprecedented political concessions. Finally, confirmation came via the Oslo channel that the PLO – though not any other Palestinian or Arab representative – would sign the DOP.

In reply to Arafat's 9 September letter of recognition, Rabin, on behalf of the Israeli government, undertook 'to recognise the PLO as the representative of the Palestinian people and commence negotiations with the PLO within the Middle East peace process ... in the light of the PLO commitments included in your letter'. These 'commitments' were, according to Arafat's text, that 'the PLO renounces the use of terrorism and other acts of violence and will assume responsibility over all PLO elements and personnel in order to ensure their compliance, prevent violations and discipline violators'. Furthermore, 'the PLO affirms that those articles of the Palestinian Covenant which deny Israel's right to exist and the provisions of the Covenant which are inconsistent with the commitments of this letter are now inoperative and no longer valid'.

In terms of the history of Palestinian nationalism, these commitments were truly epochal, but in the eyes of most Palestinians in the occupied territories they paled in significance compared to Israel's recognition of the PLO. In the West Bank and Gaza, though not in the diaspora, mass rallies and street parties erupted beneath portraits of Arafat and the black, white, green and red colours of the now no longer outlawed Palestinian flag. Even sceptics were swept up by the euphoria. 'Nothing', said PPP General Secretary Bashir Barghouti, 'can now stop the momentum leading to the establishment of an independent Palestinian state'.

Functional Autonomy

Rabin was more sober. 'We are prepared to be party to establishing a reality whereby the internal Palestinian security will be in the Palestinians' hands', he said in his defence of the DOP before the Knesset on 30 August 1993. '[L]et me re-emphasise – the security of Israelis, of settlements and Israelis both, is in our hands, with the extensive interpretation we will imbue it with. There is no commitment to the nature of the permanent solution.'

If Rabin's notion of the DOP was almost entirely security-based, there was another Israeli vision underlying it – that of Moshe Dayan and his contemporary proteges, Shimon Peres and Yossi Beilin. Dayan was Israel's minister of defence when Israel occupied the West Bank and Gaza, and he had increasingly argued that Palestinians should be granted 'functional autonomy' over all civic matters that concerned them, while Israel would keep a firm grip on the territories' resources and security. In this scenario, it ultimately mattered little what the Palestinians called their 'functional cantons' – self-government, statehood or confederation – nor which polity controlled them – the PLO, a Palestinian National Authority or Jordan. What mattered was that modalities of Israel's rule in the territories – its hegemony over 'resources and security' – would be sustained. In the Declaration of Principles, they are.

A War of Position

In an interview after Oslo, Mahmoud Abbas historicised the PLO's acceptance of the DOP as the latest of 'three stages' of Palestinian nationalism. The first, between 1948 and 1974, had been one of 'idealistic nationalism', predicated on the destruction of Israel and the recovery of Palestine as a whole. The second was the long process of internal debate, conditioned by the PLO's military defeats in Jordan and Lebanon, which began with the PLO's 1974 decision to form a 'national authority' on any area of liberated Palestinian territory and culminated in the PLO's endorsement in 1988 of a two-state solution. The current stage was of 'political realism' in which the PLO had agreed to the compromises of 'Gaza/Jericho First' and 'self-government' as the necessary means and price to realise eventual self-determination.[26]

For the opponents of Oslo, Abbas's 'realism' disguised a political defeat for the PLO that would prove to be every bit as catastrophic as its 1982 military defeat in Lebanon. For its supporters, while the DOP had closed the door on the period of armed struggle, it offered the possibility of a new political struggle, a war of position. The stakes of liberation would depend on whether Israel's security-led and 'functional' vision would prevail or whether the PLO could establish independent, national and democratic institutions inside the territories that would make the momentum toward national independence and self determination irreversible.[27]

At the time of Oslo, the optimists were in a majority. Many believed that the return of the exiled PLO leadership and cadre – including some from the opposition – could only strengthen and unify this new national struggle. But for others, Haidar Abd al-Shafi chief among them, the return of an unreconstructed PLO leadership to what, for them, was the entirely new terrain of the occupied territories was precisely the reason why he had rejected Oslo.

I always said during these last 20 months when we were negotiating that I would accept what the Israelis are offering if we ourselves were in better shape, if I had confidence that we could develop what we take into something better ... But we have neglected tending to our internal matters and consolidating our inner potential, so we are not in a position to exploit the possibilities that arise, to put our potential in the service of our cause. We lack the experience. As I see it, we lack the will.[28]

2

A Crisis of Representation

Gaza/Jericho First, as the Declaration of Principles came to be known, garnered mixed returns when Arafat finally did bring the text before the PLO's constituent bodies. In the territories there was a groundswell of support: polls in Gaza and the West Bank showed a solid 60 per cent in favour. But there was also fear that Arafat had gambled all on a presumption that, once the PLO got a toehold in the territories, a combination of popular support, cash from international donors and a Palestinian police force under his control would immeasurably improve his bargaining position vis-à-vis the Israelis and end the PLO's isolation in the region. The idea that the Israelis would not try to capitalise on the ambiguities and lacunae in the agreement betrayed, as one Palestinian observer put it, 'a catastrophic strategic ineptitude' on the PLO leader's part.[1]

From the outset, the DOP enjoyed little consensus within PLO ranks, including Arafat's own Fatah movement. Arafat managed to secure a majority of Fatah's Central Committee in favour of the deal, but opponents included such veteran leaders as Farouq Qaddumi, Hani al-Hasan and Abbas Zaki. At the PLO's Central Council, in October 1993, the 68 to 8 vote endorsement of Oslo obscured the boycott of 25 members allied with the PFLP and DFLP. In a decision condemned at the time by other Palestinians as an 'abdication of historic responsibility', the PLO's Marxist wings suspended their participation in all PLO decision-making bodies and asserted their intention to work against this 'agreement of shame'.

The 'rejectionist' case was fatally flawed by the failure to offer any viable alternative. Other, more independent Palestinian voices could not be so easily refuted. Palestine's 'national poet' Mahmoud Darwish resigned from the PLO Executive Committee, dismissing Gaza/Jericho First as 'a dangerous adventure'. The respected Palestinian academic, Edward Said, denounced the agreement as 'an embarrassment' that had reduced the PLO from a liberation movement to a 'small town council'. And Haidar Abd al-Shafi gave up his position as head of delegation on the grounds that Oslo fell 'outside the terms of the Madrid formula'.

The upshot was the PLO's worst political schism in its 30-year history. The issue was not simply the DOP, but representivity. Given the scale of the 'commitments' made to Israel in Arafat's letter, many Palestinians insisted that legitimacy could only be conferred by convening the PNC which, constitutionally, had sole veto power over the Palestinian Covenant. This, however, Arafat was reluctant to do, preferring instead to steer the DOP course away from broad-based PLO bodies like the PNC in favour of the more closely controlled Central Council and Executive Committee.

Throughout the internal PLO debate, Arafat appeared bent on avoiding any substantive discussion of the strategy that would be required to ensure that 'limited autonomy' would not preclude the possibility of statehood. Rather, he presented the agreement as a *fait accompli*, using the PLO's financial crisis as a stick to beat his truculent colleagues into line.[2] 'For every 100 reasons against the agreement', said Arafat at the Central Council, 'I can give you 300 in support of it'. He did not, however, give them. His associates were more candid. Oslo 'could lead to a Palestinian state or a catastrophic liquidation of the Palestinian cause', acknowledged Mahmoud Abbas at the same meeting.

The Crisis Within

On 25 September 1993, Arafat called on all Palestinians in the occupied territories 'to reject violence and terrorism and to return to ordinary life'. The edict was in line with the PLO leader's 'letter of recognition', and was generally understood to mean the cessation of all military operations against Israeli targets. Less clear at the time was that the call amounted to the abandonment of any strategy of nationalist mobilisation or resistance in the territories, with Fatah cadres 'inside' relegated to mounting a 'holding operation' until the PLO leadership returned. From now on, the only game in town would be the PLO/Israeli negotiations on self-rule.

Yet for many Palestinian supporters of the DOP, the agreement's potential could only be realised if it was viewed not 'as the ceiling but as the starting point for negotiations'.[3] By concentrating exclusively on the textual detail of the DOP, Arafat appeared not only to be squandering the chance to create 'national' facts on the ground; he was allowing uncontested Israeli rule in the territories.

Israel's appreciation of this one-sided cease-fire was immediate. On 26 September 1993, the IDF launched an operation in Gaza which left 17 houses destroyed, 16 arrested and the summary execution of two Hamas activists. Asked whether such actions were in the spirit of Oslo, IDF Chief of Staff Ehud Barak countered that 'the more terrorists are arrested before the IDF pull-out, the easier should be the task of the new Gaza [i.e., Palestinian] police'.[4]

These and subsequent army actions created a crisis of faith between the PLO in Tunis and its cadres inside, a dissension that the Israelis exploited to the hilt. Fatah's armed groups, such as the Fatah Hawks in Gaza and the Black Panthers in the West Bank, had agreed to cease 'actions against the occupation' on condition that the IDF would 'not come after our fighters'. In return, the army pledged a general amnesty to all 'wanted persons' who gave themselves up to the military authorities. (Fugitives from the PFLP, DFLP, Hamas and Islamic Jihad would stay 'wanted'.)

The IDF's efforts to pry apart Fatah activists from those of the rejectionist groups were doomed from the outset. On the one hand, many Fatah supporters were unconvinced of the wisdom of exposing to the Israelis the organisational structures and personal identities of what had been, by dint of the occupation, a largely underground movement. 'For this ceasefire to work', said one Fatah activist at the time, 'we are dependent on Israeli good will. This is not a good thing to be dependent on.'

Factional loyalties in the territories, moreover, are not nearly so clear-cut as the amnesty campaign presumed. They are typically layered among older loyalties, with members of the same class, region and family often belonging to different political groups. Far from nurturing Fatah into an open and united movement, a necessary condition if the movement was going to exploit the political opportunities thrown up by Oslo, Israel's tactics prompted it to implode into competing and centrifugal blocs, gravely weakening the PLO's political authority. While the PLO in Tunis stated publicly that groups like the Hawks should be disbanded or at least reined in, grassroots Fatah leaders in the West Bank and Gaza knew that to do so would be to jeopardise their own political constituencies.

On 28 November 1993, an Israeli undercover unit shot dead Ahmad Abu Rish in Gaza. Abu Rish was a former 'wanted' Fatah activist who had been given amnesty less than a week before. The impact was inflammatory: Gaza erupted in violence and the Hawks declared that they would no longer abide by any truce.

Arafat's response to this crisis of his authority was to evade it via administrative fiat. In the aftermath of Abu Rish's killing, he appointed Faisal Husseini and Zakaria Agha as Fatah's 'sole' leaders in the West Bank and Gaza. Both were from Palestine's landowning elite. The shake-up was widely interpreted to mean that, come the autonomy, it would be the older generation of Palestinian notables who would

garner the lion's share of the political spoils, not the younger constituencies of ex-prisoners, workers and students who had come to
the fore prior to, and during, the uprising.

In an atmosphere of ongoing Israeli repression and domestic
political discontent, this appointment was just about the worst signal
that Arafat could send to Fatah's rank-and-file. In December 1993, PLO
leaders in Gaza and Hebron resigned their posts. The ostensible
reasons were Arafat's 'cronyism and favouritism' in his distribution
of offices. In fact, the position of local figures like Sami Samahandana
– head of the PLO's office in Gaza and former prison activist – had
become no longer tenable. Charged with the responsibility of mediating
between Tunis and its increasingly fractious base inside, and also
between groups like the Hawks and the IDF, he and his cohorts had
failed on both counts. The Israelis were intransigent on matters
pertaining to security – which included, apparently, the right to assas-
sinate wanted Palestinians. The PLO, for its part, had conspicuously
abrogated any political role for the intifada's erstwhile young fighters.

The resignations were thus a sign that what had once been an
unifying struggle for national liberation was collapsing into a culture
of dependency on favours from Tunis. 'We were fighters', mused Samahandana on the eve of his resignation, 'now they want us to be
bureaucrats'.

The Implosion of Fatah

Palestinians viewed this turmoil in the PLO with apprehension. In
the territories, by virtue of the occupation, Palestinian civil society
had been the site not just of PLO but also of regional politics. In the
absence of any legal national authority, from 1967 onwards the PLO
and Jordan had engaged in a long war of position for hegemony,
mainly via the financing of rival social, educational and welfarist institutions. When, in 1988, Jordan renounced all political claims to the
West Bank, the PLO, particularly Fatah, assumed the greater share
of responsibility for these 'national' institutions and, through them,
for mediating the class, regional and generational contradictions that
comprised Palestinian political life.

With Oslo and the visible dissension it caused within Fatah, this
nationalist hegemony came under question. The PLO was no longer
accepted as the national arbiter of disputes over political power and
resources, but rather as a party to them. Contradictions held so long
in check by the struggle against occupation came increasingly to the
fore, and Fatah started to fracture along its faultlines. While the
degeneration had been evident since Madrid and arguably even
earlier, it accelerated with Oslo.

The upshot was a process of lawlessness and institutional breakdown throughout the territories, but especially in Gaza. The months after Oslo saw an increase in fighting over national institutions and the scarce resources they marshalled. The aim of these struggles was less the creation of new political structures to meet the challenges of self-rule than the cultivation of constituencies – refugee versus resident, urban versus rural, rich versus poor – as bases of factional and personal power.[5]

The struggle also spilled over onto the streets. In the month after Oslo, at least 12 Palestinians were killed in Gaza as 'collaborators', mainly at the hands of Hamas who used the killings to wrest power on the ground before the arrival of the Palestinian police. Fatah responded in kind, killing three 'collaborators' and indulging in a spate of kneecappings of 'suspects'. Gazans saw this turf war as a fight over who would 'police' the autonomy. 'We have stopped the armed struggle for the time being. I am now playing the part of a policeman, to supervise the population', said Fatah Hawks leader Rafat 'Abad in November 1993.

The established 'civilian' PLO leadership in Gaza denounced the violence as 'local initiatives' without covenant from Tunis, but this was by no means clear. Many Palestinians believed the Hawks had been sanctioned to assert an authority of arms as a way of preparing the street for the incoming PLO administration. 'We are now concentrating on internal matters, on building an internal security system', said Hawk leader Samir Abu Shamallah in November 1993. 'Outwardly the PLO says it is in favour of stopping the liquidations (collaborator killings)', another Hawk member said, 'but internally its orders are different'.[6]

The struggle was not just between Fatah and rival Palestinian groups but within Fatah itself. In the two months after Oslo, three prominent PLO Gaza leaders, including Fatah's foremost activist in the Strip, Asad Siftawi, were assassinated. To this day the assailants are unknown. PLO leaders at the time mused that the professionalism of the hits bore the fingerprints of Israeli settlers or rogue undercover units. Maybe. The visceral sense on the Palestinian streets, given the war that was being waged there, was that all three had been the victims of a power struggle among competing blocs within Fatah.

Dead-end Negotiations

From the outset on 13 October 1993, the PLO/Israeli negotiations set in motion by Oslo became snagged on the 'deliberate ambiguities' of the DOP, particularly the vexed issues of external security, the size of Jericho and Gaza's settlements.[7] The PLO delegation argued that there should be joint Palestinian/Israeli controls on the Egyptian and Jordanian borders; the Israelis held up the DOP stipulation that 'external relations' would remain in Israel's hands. Jericho, said Arafat, referred to a district of 390 square kilometres: for Israel it was a municipality of 25 square kilometres. Finally, Rabin insisted that the settlements in Gaza be defined as blocs rather than isolated communities. For the IDF to provide 'adequate security', Israel must retain, for the interim period, from 35 to 40 per cent of Gaza's territory.

In this initial phase the PLO also quietly accepted Israel's insistence that its security rather than international law be the basis for negotiations. The Palestinian delegation to the Madrid talks had held firm to the view that Israel abide by international legislation to which it was signatory, such as the Fourth Geneva Convention. The new PLO delegation, hamstrung by the DOP's security provisions, appeared unable or unwilling to raise the matter.

This shift was registered in debates over the emotionally charged issue of Palestinian prisoners. When the DOP was signed, Israel held around 17,000 Palestinian political prisoners in its jails, many of them interned for membership in an organisation that Rabin now recognised as 'the representative of the Palestinian people'. It swiftly became clear that the internees were going to be kept as ransom for PLO 'good behaviour', PLO amnesty for collaborators, information about Israeli soldiers 'missing in action', or even a generic 'end' to Palestinian 'violence'.

Arafat gained support in the territories for his refusal to submit to these conditions in time to sign the Gaza/Jericho agreement on 13 December 1993, the date set for Israel's withdrawal to begin. He lost that support with interest, however, in Cairo on 9 February 1994, when he finally did put pen to paper.

The February Cairo agreement is a tapestry of detail, but even a cursory reading reveals that Arafat conceded on all of Rabin's security conditions: that Israel's responsibility for 'external relations' included control of the borders; that Jericho would not grow much beyond the confines the Israelis had originally proposed; and that the Gaza settlements would remain Israeli-controlled enclaves.

This last concession Palestinians found particularly galling. The transformation of Gaza's settlements into 'blocs' in effect doubled the size of Israeli-held territory. 'Didn't the PLO negotiators realise', wrote exasperated Palestinian Central Council member Taysir Aruri, 'that by accepting these arrangements for Israeli settlements in the

Gaza Strip (the settlements most ready for dismantling), they gave them the elixir of life', and that 'they will be forced to deal in the same way with Israeli settlements in the West Bank?'.[8]

So dramatic was Arafat's climbdown in Cairo that Israeli negotiators were concerned they had pushed the PLO leader too far. One member of the Israeli team described Arafat during the negotiations as a 'pitiful figure'. Shimon Peres admitted that 'in Cairo we were largely negotiating with ourselves'. Israel's Environment Minister, Yossi Sarid, warned that a 'defeated' PLO was no more in Israel's interest than a victorious one. 'When you twist Arafat's arm in the name of security, you have to be careful not to break it. With a broken arm, Arafat won't be able to maintain control in Gaza and Jericho.'[9]

The reception in the territories to the Cairo agreement was almost uniformly hostile, and not only among the rejectionists. The PPP, up to then staunch supporters of the peace process, slammed it as 'a total surrender to the Israeli interpretation of the Oslo accords' that Arafat had made 'on his own'.[10]

Settlers

It was at this point, on 25 February 1994, that Baruch Goldstein, an Israeli settler and major in the army, decided to unload his Galili rifle in Hebron's al-Ibrahimi mosque, shooting dead 29 Palestinians at prayer. The magnitude of Goldstein's 'monstrous act' rocked both Israeli and Palestinian political establishments. But what also became evident in Hebron's bloody aftermath, at least to Palestinians in the West Bank and Gaza, was just how little Oslo had changed (and, by implication, would change) the modalities of Israel's rule.

In the eight days following the massacre, 33 Palestinians were killed by the army as protests erupted in Gaza, Jerusalem, Nablus, Ramallah and, of course, Hebron. Over one million Palestinians were confined to the West Bank and Gaza as Rabin sealed off the territories, once more sending their perilous economies into freefall. Most provocative of all, Rabin curfewed for nearly six weeks Hebron's 120,000 Palestinian residents – the victims of Goldstein's carnage – to ensure the safety of its 450 Jewish settlers. The Hebron massacre, together with the IDF's subsequent military crackdown, brought to a head what many Palestinians viewed as the fatal flaw of the whole Oslo package: its deference on the issue of Israeli settlements.

There were 269,000 Israeli settlers in the occupied territories in 1993, with 104,000 in the West Bank.[11] While many are ensconced in East Jerusalem (160,000) and in 'security settlements' along the rift of the Jordan valley, there are also 'political settlements' implanted deep into Palestinian population centres such as Gaza, Nablus and Hebron. These are the strongholds of ideological settler movements like Gush Emunim, for whom Zionism is not just a form of territorial nationalism but an eschatological imperative, one whose realisation is predicated on the expulsion of all Arabs from the land of Greater Israel. For these movements, Oslo represents nothing less than their own political obituary. They perceive Israel's commitment in the DOP to redeploy its military forces from West Bank Palestinian 'centres' during the interim period as merely a prelude to the eventual dismantling of political settlements at the permanent status talks. This, certainly, was the Palestinian perception, and a factor in their support of the DOP. 'If nothing else, Oslo has terminated the Zionist dream of a Greater Israel', said Fatah leader Marwan Barghouti.[12]

'We warned that we would foil these peace agreements on the ground', pledged a spokesperson for the Settler Council for Judea and Samaria in October 1993. 'We will now prove this.'[13] The 'proof' was an increase in settler provocations, eliciting Palestinian armed attacks which, in turn, brought down army repression and bolstered further settler actions. In December 1993, after Hamas assassinated two settlers in the West Bank, thousands of other settlers poured out onto the streets of Tel Aviv, Jerusalem and Hebron to proclaim 'days of war'. Two days later, three Palestinian workers were slain in their home in a West Bank village, a 'wanton' killing claimed by the Sword of David vigilante group allied to the Kach settler movement. Two weeks later, two settlers were killed in a Hamas ambush near Hebron, and on it continued. 'I can foresee a time', said Zvi Katzover, the head of Hebron's Kiryat Arba Settler Council, 'when a settler would take a gun, enter an Arab village and slaughter 30 to 40 Arabs'. That was just one month before Baruch Goldstein marched into al-Ibrahimi mosque.

A Missed Opportunity

For all its horror, many Palestinians were convinced that the massacre had offered the PLO an 'historic opportunity'.[14] In the West Bank, Faisal Husseini and Bashir Barghouti called for 'a reformulation of the DOP to include discussion of settlements now rather than after the interim period'. For Husseini especially, Hebron had made this not an option but a necessity. 'Israel has a choice', he said. 'It can have peace in the territories or it can have settlements in the territories. But it can no longer have both.'[15]

Arafat, however, hedged. He suspended the PLO's participation in the negotiations, demanding the relocation of 'political settlements' away from Palestinian cities. But he also played host in Tunis to 'secret' discussions with Israeli and US mediators, who implored him to resume negotiations in exchange for a 'temporary international presence' in Hebron and an unwritten Israeli pledge to speed up withdrawal in Gaza and Jericho. After initially hesitating, Arafat agreed. Instead of holding out for better DOP terms, Arafat took the word of the US and Israel over that of his own constituency.[16]

On 4 April 1994, the PLO delegation in Cairo signed a second 'Hebron' security agreement with Israel. In return, it got US support for UN Security Council Resolution 904 condemning the massacre and 160 international observers in Hebron. This Temporary International Presence in Hebron was accountable neither to the UN nor any corpus of international law, but rather to a joint Israeli/Palestinian committee and, therefore, to Israeli military orders in the territories. It was empowered, as one Palestinian put it, to 'observe the occupation'. Every other demand the PLO had touted in the wake of the massacre – international protection, the dismantling of 'political' settlements like those in Hebron, immediate discussion of the settlement issue – was surrendered.

The Cairo Agreement

The Hebron massacre did effect a change in Israeli thinking, particularly Rabin's. His strategic vision of self-rule remained sure – that the DOP offered Israel's best chance of keeping hold of the territories' resources and security as well as opening the way for peace with all of Israel's frontline Arab states. But the massacre had shown that the political development necessary to bring this about – that Arafat and the PLO take responsibility for 'internal Palestinian security' – was becoming more uncertain by the day.

To get 'Gaza out of Tel Aviv', it was necessary to get Israeli troops out of Gaza. The upsurge in violence in the territories after Hebron, particularly the gut popularity among Palestinians that greeted Hamas's subsequent revenge attacks on Israeli civilians inside the Green Line, persuaded Rabin that much more stalling on withdrawal would leave the PLO incapable of taking responsibility for the Palestinians of the West Bank and Gaza.

One incident in particular illustrated that time was short for Rabin and Arafat. On 28 March 1994, six Fatah activists were shot dead by an IDF undercover unit in Gaza's Jabalya refugee camp. The army initially claimed that the six were 'wanted' Fatah Hawks. Slowly it became clear, however, that the slain were neither Hawks nor fugitives but an 'internal security unit' within Fatah, staunchly pro-Oslo and pro-Arafat, responsible for reining in dissidents.

This grisly extra-judicial execution was, in the words of one Israeli official, 'a worst-case scenario because the PLO will claim, not without justice, that by negotiating with us it is exposed to Israeli undercover activities as well as to opposition Palestinian groups'.[17] Rabin claimed the 'accident' was due to an 'unravelling of coordination' between Fatah and the IDF. He neglected to say that this unravelling stemmed from a 'security' policy that simultaneously pursued negotiations and shoot-to-kill operations.

The Jabalya killings degraded Arafat's status even further. Members of his own Fatah movement publicly called for the end of negotiations with the Israelis. Yet its impact on the negotiations was dramatic. Now Rabin, who had hitherto dithered over every detail of the DOP, preferring to 'let the PLO sweat in Tunis', instructed his negotiators to wrap up an agreement on Gaza/Jericho First as soon as possible, so long as it contained cast-iron security guarantees for Israel.

One week after Jabalya, 49 expelled Palestinians were allowed to return to the West Bank and Gaza. These were not like the 33 ageing notables and mayors Rabin had permitted to return the previous year, largely as penitence for the Hamas expulsions. These were young, mostly Fatah grassroots leaders who had won their spurs in the territories. These were activists like Marwan Barghouti, former head of Birzeit University Student Council, and Jamal Zaqout, member of the original UNL in Gaza and a leader of the pro-Oslo Fida party. Their repatriation had been predicated on the accomplishment of one political task: to knock the PLO into some kind of shape fit for self government.[18]

On 4 May 1994, after eight months of tortuous negotiations and six months behind schedule, the agreement on Israel's military withdrawal from Gaza and Jericho was finally initialled. If Arafat was visibly – some would say theatrically – reluctant at the Cairo ceremony, this was because the Cairo agreement consecrated Israel's security-led definition of the interim period.[19] Oslo's ambiguities about Palestinian/Israeli coordination on security matters were here translated into concrete PLO commitments. In his haste to get the Palestinian National Authority (PNA) installed in Gaza and Jericho, Arafat granted the Israelis concessions on 'security' far more sweeping than anything specified in the DOP. 'The Cairo Agreement means that the Gaza Strip and Jericho will remain under the authority of the (Israeli) military', wrote Israeli political analyst, Meron Benvenisti.

> Sovereign powers of the Israeli army will not be limited to the turf of the settlements but extend over the entire territory placed under autonomy. Accordingly, the Palestinians have agreed that the

entire intricate system of military ordinances issued in the past by
Military Governors will retain its force, along with the Knesset legislation, which ... extended Israeli jurisdiction upon the settlements
and their populace, turning them ... into an inseparable part of
Israeli society.[20]

3

The Islamist Challenge

When the Oslo accords were signed, some commentators predicted that 'peace' would spell the end of any resurgent political Islam in the occupied territories, and particularly of its primary manifestation, the Islamic Resistance Movement, or Hamas.[1] Palestine's Islamists – so the argument ran – had garnered support largely as the by-product of mounting Palestinian frustration with the Madrid-founded peace process on the one hand, and the PLO's increasingly serious financial crisis and institutional paralysis on the other. Oslo would not only restore the PLO's domestic and international standing as the 'sole legitimate representative of the Palestinian people', it would replenish the movement's coffers, and so lubricate the networks of political coalitions and patronage through which legitimacy could be consolidated.

Hamas's initial reactions to the Declaration of Principles were absolute rejection, couched in terms of high treason. 'We will mobilise Palestinians in the occupied territories to destroy the agreement by force', railed an official communique in September 1993. But, in practice, Hamas's armed policy in the wake of the DOP was tactical rather than wholly destructive. In the period since Oslo, in fact, Hamas has established itself as the single largest opposition force in Palestinian society. They have done this through cleverly calibrated tactics of guerilla warfare and political alliances whose object was less to destroy the Oslo agreements than to assert an Islamist social agenda for Palestinian civil society under the changed circumstances of autonomy.

In 1989 former IDF general Aharon Yariv paid a backhanded compliment to more than two decades of Palestinian armed struggle. The PLO, he said, 'understands that the aim of any military operation is political, and that the success of such operations should be measured in political terms'.[2] A similar logic drove Hamas's military actions after Oslo. The aim was not to scupper the DOP completely, but to stall its implementation. The longer the peace dividends could be delayed in the territories, the Islamists figured, the greater the PLO's loss of support and legitimacy. It was an accurate prognosis.

Hamas's actions, like the December 1993 ambush of Colonel Mintz, coordinator of the IDF's undercover units in the Gaza Strip, or the murder of General Security Service operative Noam Cohen, killed by one of his own informers in the West Bank in February 1994, generated huge kudos on the Palestinian street. They also struck fear into the Israeli security establishment. On the Mintz hit, army sources were quoted saying that, in terms of professionalism, Fatah 'had achieved nothing remotely resembling it during the 26 years [sic] of its existence'.[3]

The targets were Israeli, but Hamas's political sights were fixed firmly on the PLO leadership, particularly Arafat. No Palestinian leader could possibly condemn the killing of a Mintz or a Cohen, and Arafat pointedly refrained from doing so. His dilemma was that whereas for the Israelis silence was tantamount to collusion, for Palestinians any public disavowal implied collaboration. The PLO leader was thus damned if he did speak and damned if he didn't.

A similar logic was at play with Hamas's actions to avenge the Hebron massacre, especially their revived penchant for hitting Israeli civilians inside the Green Line. On 6 April 1994, a West Bank Palestinian rammed a car full of explosives into a crowded bus station in the Israeli town of Afula, killing eight and wounding 40 others. In a statement claiming responsibility, Hamas said that ending the attacks was 'conditional on Israeli settlers quickly leaving the West Bank and Gaza' – a sentiment with which polls showed 88 per cent of Palestinians in the territories concurred. But if killing soldiers and settlers compromised Arafat, killing Israelis 'inside sovereign Israel' lit the fire beneath Rabin.

In a survey published in January 1994, 70 per cent of Israelis said they would consider 'Palestinian autonomy a failure if terrorists continue to murder Jews'. Domestic opinion thus usually compelled the rote demand that Arafat do something to curb 'fundamentalist terror'. The problem for Rabin was that he knew that the PLO leader was powerless to stop Hamas, not just because of 'internal constraints' but because such impotence was written into the Oslo accords. There it states categorically that Israel retains responsibility for the 'external security' of the 'autonomous areas' – in other words, for Israel and Israelis. Hamas, of course, knew this too. 'If Hamas launched an attack against Israelis in Gaza during the autonomy, this would undoubtably cause problems for the PLO leadership', said one leading Islamist. 'But what if Hamas were to hit Israelis in Tel Aviv? What has the PLO to do with the protection of Tel Aviv?'[4]

Rabin typically responded to such 'provocations' by closing off the West Bank and Gaza, rounding up hundreds of Hamas 'suspects' and launching massive punitive raids to hunt down 'Muslim extremists'. Yet each successive crackdown only chipped away at the PLO leader's standing in the territories, and Rabin's conviction that 'only Arafat' could run the self-rule regime.

The upshot of Hamas's military strategy after Oslo was ably summed up by Israeli journalist Danny Rubinstein. 'Hamas's terrorist activities contain two main political messages', he wrote in December 1993. 'The first – to Arafat and the PLO – is do not dare ignore us; the second – to the state of Israel – is that negotiations with the PLO do not constitute the final word and that Hamas must also be taken into account.'[5]

The Olive Branch

However 'rejectionist' its public face, Hamas's stance vis-à-vis the other PLO factions after Oslo was essentially conciliatory, signalling that the Islamists were fully cognisant of the new political realities raised by self-rule. In January 1994, Hamas announced its formal enlistment in the Palestinian Forces Alliance, a Damascus-based grouping of ten Palestinian movements opposed to the DOP and including the PLO's PFLP and DFLP. Hamas had been in talks with the Fronts since Oslo, but these had snagged on wrangles over the weight of each organisation's representation in the alliance.[6]

Hamas's principal motive for joining this unprecedented nationalist-Islamist bloc was tactical. On the one hand, it worked with the Fronts to notch up such notable victories as Birzeit University's 1993 Student Council elections when, for the first time in 20 years, a Fatah-backed coalition lost out to the rejectionists.[7] On the other, it ditched the Fronts whenever it saw no electoral need for them – as in the Engineers' elections in Gaza, where Hamas stood with Islamic Jihad to tie with pro-Oslo nationalists. Both Birzeit and the engineers had historically been bastions of Fatah support.

Participation in the Alliance also allowed Hamas to drop some of the more offensive and unpopular features of its social agenda in the name of Palestinian unity. The months after Oslo witnessed a visible relaxation of Hamas's strictures against manifestations of 'un-Islamic' behaviour, such as Palestinian women going unveiled or families going to the beach 'at a time of national suffering and martyrdom', in favour of a more pragmatic line maximising political rather than sectarian support. It was, of course, supremely ironic that in their desire to avoid 'giving Arafat cover', the PLO opposition fronts had given cover to the Islamists, ideologically their greatest foe.

Most Palestinians in the territories feared the jockeying of the Damascus-led rejectionists less than they did strife between Fatah and Hamas. A deft mix of clear political direction and discipline on the part of both leaderships in the period between the signing of the DOP and the installation of the PNA kept this nightmare scenario largely at bay. In September 1993, PLO and Hamas prisoners signed a pact banning inter-Palestinian violence to resolve political disagreements over the DOP. Hamas leader Aziz Rantisi declared that the job of Islamists was 'to fight against any confrontation between supporters and opponents of the PLO–Israeli agreement'.[8]

Apart from one or two street skirmishes, both cadres adhered to the line of peaceful coexistence, even in relation to potentially explosive issues such as the fate of collaborators and the role of the Palestinian police. While Hamas repeatedly warned the PLO delegation not to give amnesty to collaborators in exchange for Israeli promises to release prisoners, Yasin also implied that, as long as the PNA 'settles accounts with the criminals', Hamas would 'not intervene in those affairs'.[9] A like approach held with the police. In October 1993 after an ambush near a Gaza settlement in which Hamas guerrillas, dressed as Israelis, killed two IDF reservists, Hamas released a video tape pledging peace with the Palestinian police 'unless they raise their guns against us'. On the eve of the police's entry into Gaza and Jericho, even this vaguely menacing tone had been moderated to the point of fraternity. 'We welcome the Palestinian security forces as brothers', said Gaza Islamist Ibrahim Yazouri in May 1994.

This new conciliationism was perhaps most evident in Hamas's shifting perceptions of the centrality of the PLO to Palestinian politics – nationalist and Islamist alike. Whereas Palestinian Islamism had evolved largely as a reaction to the PLO's secular nationalism, after Oslo, Islamists took pains to stress the patriotism of their opposition. 'It would not be in the Palestinian interest', said Islamist intellectual Bassam Jarrar, 'to have the PLO fall apart'.[10] Rantisi mused that Hamas sought not the 'downfall of the PLO' but rather that its 'structure and shape be redefined on a democratic basis'.

The Ballot Box

From the moment Arafat shook Rabin's hand, most Islamists understood that Oslo was politically irreversible. 'We can't stand up and say to people we want the occupation to stay', said Islamist journalist Khalid Amayreh in September 1993. 'That would be irrational. You have to be realistic or the current will move you aside.' The issue for Hamas was: what would its place be in self-rule, and what would its attitude be towards elections for the Palestine National Authority .

The line of the Islamist–Marxist alliance was to have no truck with 'any elections or bodies to be established in compliance with the Gaza/Jericho accord'. It was clear from the outset that Hamas was hardly going to be bound by this stricture. As early as October 1993, Yasin reportedly said that Hamas would take part in elections 'because it wanted to have influence on the daily lives of Palestinians in the occupied territories'.[11]

Hamas's position on PNA elections has swung between these two poles, suggesting a strong debate within the movement. While many Hamas supporters believe that their participation in self-rule would 'lend the DOP a credibility it does not have', others point to the electoral successes Islamist blocs have scored in an array of Palestinian professional associations across the territories.[12] If they took part in self-rule elections, they argue, they would not defeat the PLO but they would almost certainly be the strongest opposition party. Their political, social and legal leverage would be such that the PLO would have to accommodate them or ignore them at its peril.

On the PNA's installation in July 1994, Hamas struck a compromise, most clearly spelled out by Bassam Jarrar and Gaza spokesperson Mahmoud Zahar. Both stated that while Hamas would not initially participate in elections 'born of the DOP', it would stand for institutions of 'Palestinian public interest' such as the municipalities and professional associations. Other Islamists have stated that Hamas's eventual participation in the PNA will depend on the extent of independent legislative power it enjoys. Hamas's place in the self-rule, in other words, was going to be oppositional but not mutinous.

A Loyal Opposition?

In April 1994, the military wings of Fatah and Hamas in Gaza signed an accord of non-belligerence. The two movements promised a moratorium on collaborator killings, to end all 'defamatory campaigns' between them, and to cut back separately-called strike days 'to lighten the economic burden of our people'. While Palestinians in the territories breathed a collective sigh of relief, news of the pact sent Israeli leaders, to borrow Rabin's parlence, 'spinning like propellers', enraged that the liaison made no commitment to ending Hamas's armed attacks against Israelis. 'It is out of the question', thundered Rabin, 'that the PLO should even think of achieving cooperation [with Hamas] on the basis of attacking Israelis'.

These outpourings, necessary for public relations, were disingenuous. Not only had Israeli negotiators like Amnon Shahak long foreseen that Hamas would have no option but to join the autonomy; the Israeli government flew numerous kites enticing it to do so. Four days after the pact was announced, IDF Commander Doron Almog met with Hamas leader Muhsein Abu Ata to discuss the Israeli–PLO agreement and the new Fatah–Hamas rapproachment. The next day Shimon Peres floated the idea that his government would 'sit down with Hamas' and release its prisoners if it renounced violence and started 'down the road to negotiations'.

For PLO activists in the territories the meaning of the Fatah–Hamas agreement was transparent: Hamas, finally and publicly, had accepted self-rule as fact and was about to set out its store for the new politics it augured. But what does Hamas want? This is not such an easy question, since political Islam in Palestine, like the Islamist resurgence elsewhere in the region, is homogeneous neither in its constituencies nor in its aims.

The bulk of Hamas's support in Gaza and the West Bank is drawn from socially conservative sectors for whom the ideology of secular nationalism is an apology for the materialism, corruption and moral permissiveness of the region's ruling regimes. The attraction of Islamism lies in its austere moral code, with its emphasis on pious conduct and the application of Islamic values to all civic spheres. Thus for Islamist religious figures such as Sheikh Jamal Salim, the 'red lines' governing Hamas's place in the autonomy are not so much the incendiary political questions of Jewish settlements and Jerusalem as 'freedom of expression in the mosques and the right to speak about the religious point of view not only in religion but in politics, social values, economics, etc.'.

Another red line is the Islamists' insistence that there be a total separation between existing Islamic courts in the territories which cover all laws pertaining to personal status such as marriage, inheritance and divorce, and the PNA's new Ministry of Justice which will presumably follow secular law. For Hamas, the preservation and consolidation of *shari'a* over this private sphere of civil society, and with it the social reproduction of the Palestinian family as the 'basic unit' of society, affords perhaps the greatest prize of self-rule. It ensures, said Jarrar, 'the guarantee of Palestinians' human rights as Muslims'.[13]

But these Hamas demands now have to be accommodated with more overtly nationalist priorities. With its turn to active national struggle in the intifada, Hamas succeeded in drawing into its sphere increasing numbers of younger, more militant cadres. For these generations, Islam means not just *shari'a*, but also national liberation from Israeli occupation. For them, Hamas's message is enshrined less in the sage wisdom of figures like Shaikh Yasin than in the exemplary military actions of Islamic Jihad and Hizballah, and the daring operations of the Izzadin al-Qassim brigades.

The presence of this younger strata in Hamas signals not the demise of nationalist ideology, but its transformation, imbuing it rather with a religious soul that secularism is felt to lack. Hamas accommodated the PLO's secular nationalism ideologically by inventing for it an Islamist tradition that is now been experienced as an integral part of Palestinian national identity, especially by those generations politically forged by the uprising.[14]

Armed Struggle

Whether this mix of social conservatism and radical nationalism can be contained within the same movement is the challenge self-rule has thrown down to Hamas. Unlike most of the PLO factions, Hamas operates politically as a broad alliance whose line at any point is determined by consensus. On the eve of the PNA's establishment in Gaza and Jericho, the consensus was set out in an 'important official statement' issued by the head of Hamas's Political Department, Musa Abu Marzuq. Hamas, he said, would offer a 'ceasefire [*hodna*] with the occupation' if Israel withdrew to its 1967 borders, disarmed all settlers as a preliminary to dismantling all settlements, released Palestinian prisoners and permitted elections to a 'sovereign body' that would represent all Palestinians and possess the authority to 'define Palestinian self determination', including the legislative power to repeal or amend the DOP.

Israel, of course, would reject any 'truce' under these conditions. But this was not the point. Rather, Hamas was highlighting the deficiencies of the DOP (which, in its textual commitments, guarantees none of these demands) while also making a pitch for mainstream Palestinian opinion. The references to the '1967 borders' and 'settlements' indicate a *de facto* recognition of Israel, and so place Hamas squarely within contemporary Palestinian nationalist discourse.

Marzuq's pronouncement spurred disquieted murmurings from Hamas's more militant cadres, but it was ambiguous enough to appease moderates and radicals alike. For 'realists' like Khalid Amayreh, the new consensus intimated Hamas's eventual reversion to its 'ideological fundamentals by placing more emphasis on its eternal bedrock theme – Islam is the solution – and less on its ultimate theo-political objective, the complete liberation of Palestine and the establishment of an Islamic state'.[15] In this scenario, the attitude to Israel – as stated by leading Islamists such as Shaikh Ahmad Bitawi – becomes pragmatic to the point of defeatist. 'The Islamic tendency has reached the conclusion', he said in April 1994,

> that it is no longer possible to halt the [DOP] negotiations, since the US, which rules our region, is pushing towards [their] completion. But the negotiations with Israel must grant the Palestinians' minimal rights, such as the 1967 borders, and at this time they will be satisfied with that. The continuation of the solution of the Palestinian problem will be in the hands of future generations.[16]

Another Hamas leader admitted that for 'realist' Islamists in the territories there is now 'only one taboo, and that is recognition of Israel ... anything else is permitted'. For radicals, however, Marzuq's statement meant what it said – that the national, including armed, struggle would go on until Israel fulfilled Palestinians' minimal rights of withdrawal, prisoner releases and sovereignty.

If Hamas wants to return to its 'ideological fundamentals', it is going to have to reach some sort of working accommodation with the PNA. It is clear that no accommodation is feasible – none, at any rate, that would survive the long arm of Israel or the PNA's security forces – without a commitment from the Islamists to end the armed struggle, at least in those areas under autonomy. Jarrar said that 'Hamas will cease military operations when it sees it to be in its best interest to do so.'[17] The debate hinges on the timing of 'best interest'. The realists say it should now be to foreclose any 'fractricidal' conflict with the PNA. The radicals say it should be once Israel withdraws militarily from the occupied territories.

In October 1994, in response to a crackdown on Hamas supporters by both Israel and the PNA, Hamas's military wing unleashed an unprecedented onslaught on Israeli civilian and military targets. Three separate operations – a random gun attack in Jerusalem, the kidnapping and killing of an Israeli soldier in the West Bank, and a bomb planted on an autobus in downtown Tel Aviv – left a toll of 25 Israelis dead and over 50 injured. The demands that accompanied these actions were nationalist rather than Islamist: to Israel, that it immediately release 200 Palestinian prisoners, including and especially Shaikh Yasin; and to the PNA, that it cease supplying 'information ... on our *mujahidin* [holy fighters] ... to the Zionist intelligence and occupation authorities'.

This escalation of the armed struggle stretched the Islamist consensus to breaking point. Amayreh said that the Tel Aviv bombing in particular 'would be detrimental to Hamas and its popularity' and that 'some people identified with Hamas will distance themselves from the perpetrators'. But a Hamas leader in Gaza, Shaikh Ahmed Baher, justified the operations as 'legitimate ... as long as the occupation continues'.

Perhaps the only solution, one currently under intense discussion among Islamist circles, is the formation of an Islamist political party for the 'new situation' of autonomy. This would be affiliated with Hamas as the political or public wing of the movement. It would focus on promulgating 'Islamic values' for Palestinian civil society, while Hamas's military arm would be kept in reserve, able, in Zahar's words, to pursue its 'own independent policy and strategy'.

As another Hamas leader, Ismail Haniyeh, implies, even this 'independence' would have to be 'rationalised'. 'I think the Islamic movement will carry out military operations only in response to blatant Israeli aggression against our people', he said. 'And the scale of the attacks will be determined by the level of popular support for such a strategy. A political party is crucial for dealing with the new situation [of] resisting the occupation, but avoiding a showdown with the PNA.'[18]

The Challenge

It is too close to call Hamas's ultimate future course, since this is intimately bound up with the course of the PNA. If the Islamists do metamorphose into a loyal opposition, it will come at a price, probably Hamas's influence in Palestinian civil society. The alternative, Hamas's continuation as an active military organisation, is liable to provoke either an extremely authoritarian form of self-rule or civil war.[19]

In the longer term, the prospect of an emergent Islamist culture in the occupied territories carries many risks for the Palestinian national struggle. Like other variants of political Islam, Hamas embodies an apparent conundrum. It is an entirely modernist political movement, deploying mass modes of social mobilisation and organisation to propagate its ideology and garnering a deserved reputation of financial probity, community service and military finesse. Yet its archaic and prohibitive interpretation of Islam cannot meet the political, social and economic challenges raised by self-determination. It further risks bequeathing an anti-democratic and sectarian identity that will ultimately corrode the very foundations of contemporary Palestinian nationalism. In the opinion of the Palestinian political thinker Jamil Hilal, formerly with the Democratic Front, Hamas's rejection of secularism and implicit contempt for 'territorial' nationalism threatens precisely that modernist political and cultural identity that

> has been one of the strongest and most militant tools in Palestinians' fight against Zionist sectarian ideology ... as well as one of the strongest safeguards against attempts to assimilate, dominate and settle Palestinians in the diaspora.[20]

If Hamas commands increasing support among Palestinians since Oslo, this is not due to any mass turn to faith. It is rather the consequence of two interrelated crises of PLO nationalist ideology and practice: first, a political crisis of representation, aggravated by an increasingly unaccountable, authoritarian and autocratic national leadership; and second, an ideological crisis over the social agenda and content of any future Palestinian polity. It is not, as Hamas's ubiquitous slogans would have it, that 'peace with Jews is blasphemy' or that 'Islam is the solution'. Rather, such sentiments have popular (and populist) resonance because they beg the cardinal but yet unanswered questions: What kind of peace? And if not an Islamic nation, then what kind of nation?

4

The Political Economy of Self-rule

Palestinian and Israeli negotiators in Paris signed the Protocol on Economic Relations between Israel and the PLO on 29 April 1994. The Paris agreement regulates economic relations between the state of Israel and the autonomous Palestinian areas for the duration of the interim period, initially in Gaza and Jericho and, subsequently, in the rest of the West Bank. While the protocol is formally subordinate to the DOP and the Cairo security agreements, many Palestinians consider it ultimately more significant since the strategic question of the autonomy's future economic relations with Israel should underpin any Palestinian vision for self-determination.

This importance is acknowledged in the protocol's preamble. 'The two parties', it says, 'view the economic domain as one of the cornerstones in their mutual relations with a view to enhance their interest in the achievement of a just, lasting and comprehensive peace'. It was also reflected in the rare light of PLO/Israeli unanimity that greeted the protocol's endorsement. There is 'nothing but an independent Palestinian state behind this agreement', said chief PLO economics negotiator in Paris, Ahmad Qrei, while his Israeli counterpart, David Brodet, announced that the Israelis had given the Palestinians a 'big present'. Shimon Peres was more honest, if more cryptic, when he said that what the entire Oslo package portends between the Israelis and the Palestinians is 'a political divorce and an economic marriage'.

The Paris Protocol

A close reading of the agreement reveals the 'marriage' to be rather asymmetrical. Despite its insistence that the autonomy's economic relations with Israel will be governed by the principles of 'reciprocity, equity and fairness', the protocol barely refers to the Israeli economy at all. Rather, its main aim is to lay 'the groundwork for strengthening the economic base of the Palestinian side'.

Thus the pledge of the free flow of labour between Israel and the autonomy is hedged by the rider which gives both parties 'the right to determine ... the extent and conditions of labour movement into the area'. What this means in practice is that Israel can grant Pales-

35

tinians access to employment in its economy, and can suspend it by closing off the autonomous areas on security grounds. Given that 25 per cent of the territories' GNP is derived from wages earned in Israel, this represents a major constraint on the economic independence of the PNA.

Similarly, the protocol grants Palestinians permission to decide customs policy and procedures for a total of 526 imports from 'Arab, Islamic and other countries'. Palestinians can import basic foodstuffs, certain processed foods, essential consumer products and some capital equipment for textile, construction and agricultural sectors.

These are precisely the peripheral sectors that Israeli policymakers have targeted as amenable to Palestinian development in the territories, since they complement Israeli economic scenarios. Should the Palestinians choose to import items that fall outside of the agreed lists – raw materials for industrial or technological development, for instance – they will be subject to a PLO/Israeli Joint Economic Committee (JEC) whose remit is to assess 'consumption, production, investment and external trade' on the basis of 'Palestinian market needs' (there is no mechanism in the protocol for assessing Israel's market needs). The JEC has powers to set qualitative and quantitative limits on imports as a 'defence' against goods from neighbouring countries flooding the Israeli market. Peres's 'marriage', in other words, is less one between equals than a political arrangement in which the Palestinians have negotiated a partnership with the Israelis for developing their economic affairs.[1]

The Palestinian Debate

If the Paris protocol preserves the unequal relationship between Israel and the territories, it does represent a new order. Whereas under occupation the Palestinian economy was in thrall to a myriad of Israeli military stipulations, the Paris agreement lifts these and pledges open economic borders between the two parties. In agriculture, for instance, Palestine will enjoy a 'free movement of produce, free of customs and import taxes'. In theory, the agreement is consonant with the PLO's own commitment to promote 'a free market economy' under self-rule which 'guarantees the cardinal role for the private sector'.[2]

But these commitments do not exist in a vacuum. Their contexts are the political and security modalities set down in the Oslo and Cairo agreements. At stake is whether the PLO's embrace of a neoliberal economic policy is compatible with its political desire to develop a genuinely independent economic sector for self-rule. The Palestinian debate hinges on this issue: whether Paris provides an opportunity to lay the basis of economic sovereignty – the right of Palestinians to control the economic affairs of their own nation – or augurs the final incorporation of the territories as adjuncts of the Israeli economy.[3]

Palestinian economist George Abed is cautiously optimistic. He argues that in at least three crucial economic areas there are elements of sovereignty 'more favourable to the Palestinians than one would have expected from a careful reading of the DOP'.[4]

The protocol gives the PNA the right to define its own import and tariff policy over a wide range of commodities. Even if the Palestinians have to import many required products under an Israeli customs regime, the revenues they generate could still be mobilised to fund independent national institutions in the territories and so set in motion a process of state formation. In the area of money and banking, also, the protocol enables the PNA to set up its own Palestinian Monetary Authority, with powers to license and regulate banks in the territories and manage financial reserves. Even in the confines of 'limited autonomy', such powers offer a degree of hitherto unprecedented Palestinian independence in the fields of investment and monetary policy. Finally, the protocol's endorsement of the principle of 'free trade' between Israel and the territories means that Palestinians are now 'able to export almost everything without limits', with the exception of six agricultural goods where the restrictions will be lifted gradually over a four-year period. The boost this is expected to give Palestinian industry – which comprised only 10 per cent of the territories' GDP in 1987 and has fallen since – should allow the PNA to at least begin establishing a local production base in the territories.

These scenarios are predicated on the PNA being able to fulfil certain infrastructural conditions. Chief among them, said Abed, is to create the 'legal and regulatory environment' necessary to stimulate private investment in the territories; to mobilise donor money, private Palestinian capital and the Palestinian population in a national campaign to implement a development programme to produce jobs 'at home'; and to set up a working fiscal system that will generate the revenue needed to fund the new Palestinian administration and public services.

The vision underlying Abed's prognoses is that the Palestinian economy develop in tandem with Israel's rather than attempting to disengage from it. Any sudden de-linking of the economies would require major structural readjustments on the part of the Palestinian economy, resulting in a decline in living standards and, in the short term at least, onerous competition with countries like Jordan and

Egypt which already have an infrastructure in place, cheaper labour costs and a more advanced market structure.[5] Abed also cites possible benefits from maintaining 'the special relationship' with Israel, such as indirect taxation in the form of value-added tax (VAT). 'The [VAT] system in the West Bank and Gaza will have to remain fairly close to that in Israel', Abed writes,

> but in the end this may not be such a bad thing. Israel has one of the most efficient and developed VAT systems in the world, and if the Palestinians were to run their system as efficiently they could cover a substantial portion – perhaps more than half – of their current budgetary requirements from VAT alone. This would not only mobilise domestic resources and dispense with the need for foreign budgetary support, but could also permit a reduction in the income tax burden, especially on lower income groups.[6]

An optimistic reading of Paris is thus contained in the notion of a Palestinian–Israeli partnership based on political cooperation and free trade. Transforming limited autonomy into economic sovereignty will take Palestinian resourcefulness and ingenuity and require generous and sustained support from the international community. Above all, it supposes enormous good will and flexibility on the part of Israel, particularly that it yield its current *de facto* sovereignty over Palestinian economic resources.

Critics of the protocol argue that political dependency cannot but mask economic dependency, albeit in a new guise. For them, the freer the Palestinian market, the greater will be Israel's economic domination of it. This pessimistic reading of Paris rests less on its textual detail than on recent Israeli practice in three Palestinian economic sectors and on the essentially neo-colonial vision that drives it.

Subcontracting. In the aftermath of the second Gulf war, Israel perceived a 'security need' to staunch the flow of Palestinian labour across the Green Line, running then at around 30,000 workers from Gaza and 180,000 from the territories altogether. The result has been not so much to lessen territories' chronic dependency on the Israeli economy than to re-structure the relations of that dependency. In place of 'the daily migration of mass Palestinian labour', said Gaza economist Salah Abd al-Shafi, 'the vehicle [of dependency] is a system of subcontracting between Palestinian capital and sectors of Israeli capital'.[7]

By the time of the Paris agreement, no more than 65,000 workers from the territories were employed in Israel on any given day. The effect, especially in Gaza, has been a burgeoning 'black' economy, where Palestinians trade between themselves or set up small sub-contracting outfits whose business is exclusively geared to Israeli firms. Israeli contractors export raw materials for assembly by Gazan sub-contractors, who then export the products back across the Green Line for retail in Israel. Due to Israel's closure and labour substitution policies, and the massive structural unemployment these caused, Palestinian labour in Gaza was not only cheaper than Israeli labour in Israel; it was also cheaper than Palestinian labour in Israel.

Far from cracking down on this informal – and illegal – economic activity, the Israeli occupation authorities have cultivated it. In 1991, they issued Military Order 105 which, for the first time, permitted free Palestinian investment in Gaza. The new licensing policy benefited mainly those Palestinian subcontractors in peripheral sectors – furniture-making, textiles, food production – of the Israeli economy, and so did not threaten any structural competition.

This 'freeing-up' was significant, in light of the later Oslo and Paris agreements. It signalled that from now on the rules for economic activity in the territories were going to be set less by military diktat than by the surrounding Israeli dominated economic environment. Israel was quietly shifting from direct economic subjugation of the territories to a 'dominant integration' of them – in other words, from colonialism to neo-colonialism.[8]

Agriculture. This integrationist thrust has been very clear vis-à-vis Palestinian agriculture. True, the Paris protocol allows Palestinians to freely export their farm produce to Israel, but Israeli measures in the last five years have incorporated the Palestinian agricultural sector as an intrinsic part of the Israeli agricultural sector. The mechanisms of this incorporation can be shown through the example of citrus production in Gaza.

Citrus is Gaza's single biggest income earner, historically, with exports to Europe and the Gulf countries. Due to a series of punitive measures imposed by the Israelis since 1991, the quantity of arable citrus land in Gaza has shrunk from 75,000 dunums to 53,000 dunums. Israel's purpose is less confiscatory than politico-economic, decoupling Gaza producers' trade with other economies as a means of locking it more securely into its own. The result is that of the 9000 tonnes of citrus harvested in Gaza in 1993, 90 per cent was sold to Israeli juice factories.[9]

At the same time, the territories' agricultural trade with Arab countries has declined. Whereas in 1984 the volume of trade in fruit and vegetables between the territories and Jordan was 244,000 tonnes, during the 1990s the average was 44,000. Even with the removal of Israeli prohibitions, said Palestinian economist Hisham Awartani,

Palestinian agricultural producers 'cannot hope for more than modest exports to Jordan and other Arab markets. In contrast, Palestinians can possibly enjoy ample opportunities in the Israeli market, should restrictions on entry to that market be lifted and subsidy policies in Israel be abolished.'[10]

Industry. Since 1967, precisely to forestall the possibility of an independent economic basis for Palestinian self-determination, industry in the territories had been systematically de-developed by Israel. But in the run-up to Oslo, there was a shift in Israeli policy. Between 1991 and 1993, Israel began the construction of industrial parks in Gaza and the West Bank modelled on similar projects set up in countries like Mexico and Taiwan.[11] The thinking behind this was that, since the cost of creating an industrial infrastructure for the territories as a whole would be prohibitive, Israel should focus on enabling 'pockets of infrastructure' geared to Palestinian industry alone and situated in small zones. The capital would be supplied by Palestinian, Israeli and international sub-contractors, but tied to main contractors inside Israel. The attraction would be the mass availability of cheap Palestinian labour. 'If Palestinian workers can no longer get jobs in Israel', said Shimon Peres in November 1994, 'we must create the conditions that will bring the jobs to the workers'.

An Unlevel Playing Field

Both the optimistic and pessimistic readings of the protocol acknowledge that, in the short term, self-rule can only consolidate Israel's hold over the territories' economy. For optimists, the spur such integration will give to developing and modernising the Palestinian economy will lay the bases of economic sovereignty providing the PNA can set in place the right infrastructural conditions. The pessimists argue that independent economic development is conditional on the PNA wresting a degree of political sovereignty now, an option precluded by the DOP and the PNA's largely uncritical embrace of free trade principles. 'If the PNA wanted to pursue a policy of genuine, or even partial, disengagement from the Israeli economy', Salah Abd al-Shafi explains,

> it would have to offer Palestinian farmers, businessmen, and sub-contractors a real economic alternative. But if, as the PNA and Israel say, this must be left to the free market, then this class will obviously choose the Israelis. First, because the mutual relations are already in place and, second, because, come the peace, Israeli contractors can guarantee them authentic export markets.[12]

A similar argument holds with the PNA's currently unproblematic commitment to 'open borders'. Given the grossly uneven relationships between the Israeli and Palestinian economies, the borders will be 'open' for Israel to penetrate Arab markets but 'closed' to the Palestinians to trade in any market other than Israel's. With self-rule this will be realised less by military sanction than by economic imperative. 'If there is one point that unites all shades of Israeli political opinion about the DOP', said Salah Abd al-Shafi,

> it is [that] there must be open borders between Israel and the autonomy. While direct taxation can be in the hands of the PNA, they say, indirect taxation will have to be standardised. But if Palestinians are made to buy and sell at Israeli prices, we may as well forget Jordan or any other Arab market for that matter. And this trade disadvantage would be reinforced if, after the DOP, there is peace and economic normalisation between Israel and the Arabs. Gaza, for example, simply cannot compete with an economy that in terms of GNP is ten times its own size. As with most free markets, this is not a level playing field.[13]

The Paris agreement specifies that as long as Israel has a VAT rate of 17 per cent, the PNA must set its rate at between 15 and 16 per cent. This in itself is likely to make Palestinian products structurally uncompetitive vis-à-vis Arab markets. Uncompetitiveness is already virtually ensured because Palestinian wage levels are pegged to Israeli wage levels rather than levels in other Arab countries. This 'overpricing' is the fruit of the unique colonial relationship that has been structured between Israel and the territories, where Gaza and the West Bank serve not only as tributaries of cheap labour for Israel, but provide its second largest consumer market. There is a line below which Palestinian wages cannot fall because Palestinians in the territories must have enough money in their pockets to purchase Israeli goods at Israeli prices. Such structural defects are unlikely to be remedied under self-rule, since the PNA will not have anything like the revenues at its disposal to subsidise Palestinian products competitively. Nor, under Paris, will they have the capacity to diversify production.

The Israeli economy, on the other hand, does have these capacities and, given economic normalisation with its frontline Arab states, will deploy them to penetrate these and other Arab markets. Palestinian capital's role is thus likely to be less that of a competitor than of a junior partner for Israel's economic expansionism.

Capital and Labour

Israel's strategic aim has been to achieve a higher degree of economic integration with the Arab world, to gain greater access to Arab markets, and to breach the 46-year-old Arab economic boycott of Israel. For Israeli capital, breaking the boycott affords the greatest prize of peace with the Palestinians, particularly if it augurs the elimination of the so called secondary and tertiary boycotts in which foreign firms with major trade relations with Arab countries are penalised for trading with Israel.

With the Oslo and Paris agreements, a fraction of the PLO leadership has appeared to buy into this scenario, with its promise, at best, for a minor place in the region's new economic order. This means that Palestine's economy is likely to be built in coalition with Israeli capital rather than independently of it in any confederation with Arab economies.

According to Israeli economic analyst Asher Davidi, the articles in the protocol covering industry, agriculture, taxation and labour are positions that had been enthusiastically endorsed by key sectors of Israeli capital. The objective was summed up by Hilel Sheinfeld, Israel's Coordinator of Operations in the territories: his goal during the self-rule, he said, 'is to integrate the economy of the territories into the Israeli economy'.[14]

The political form of this integration is ultimately less significant than its economic dividends. 'It's not important whether there will be a Palestinian state, autonomy or a Palestinian/Jordanian federation', said the former president of the Israeli Industrialists' Association, Dov Lautman. 'The economic borders between Israel and the territories must remain open.'[15]

Given the constraints laid down by the Oslo, Cairo and Paris agreements, the Israeli vision is likely to prevail. If so, most Palestinians in the West Bank and Gaza are going to remain, in economic terms, substantially where they are.

There are likely to be two distinct economic phases for self-rule. In the short term, Israel will maintain its relative economic siege of the West Bank and Gaza that it has imposed since the Gulf war. While the ostensible reason will be 'security', the economic imperative will be to preserve the territories' vast pool of cheap labour to attract investment from Palestinian, Israeli and international capital and so to consolidate the new economic arrangements articulated by Oslo and Paris but actually set in place previously. Closure remains Israel's most lethal bargaining chip in future negotiations with the PLO, over the content of self-rule and over a permanent settlement. This is what Hisham Awartani calls Israel's 'sword over the Palestinians' neck' – the 25 to 30 per cent of the territories' GNP derived from Palestinian revenues earned in Israel.

In the longer term, if the agreement sticks, the closure will be quietly relieved, allowing between 50,000 and 70,000 Palestinian workers to fetch for their living inside the Green Line. In the first phase, structural unemployment levels will hover around their current rates of 50 per cent in Gaza and 25 per cent in the territories overall. In the second, the rates will stabilise at around 20 per cent in Gaza and lower still in the West Bank. The political impact, said Salah Abd al-Shafi, will probably have been enough for Israel to have bought the peace: 'Israel figures – perhaps accurately – that the better off certain Palestinians become economically, the more the national question will subside. ... The dispensation strengthens our economic dependency on Israel because it removes some of our political or national grievances against it.'[16]

If what Oslo and Paris harbours is the final incorporation of the territories' economy into the Israeli economy, this is occurring precisely during a period when, as Israel moves from an industrial to a post-industrial or technological mode of production, mass Palestinian labour is becoming structurally less important to it. Relocated in the West Bank and Gaza, this labour will become peripheralised in sectors such as furniture-making, textiles and food production or, in Israel, a semi-employed informal sector to be absorbed and shed as the Israeli market dictates, especially in the casual but labour-intensive construction and agricultural sectors.

Palestinian workers, under self-rule, will remain what they have become after 27 years under occupation: an underclass. An underclass provides cheap and flexible labour during periods of rapid technological change, and it acts as a buffer, absorbing the worst shocks of economic restructuring and cushioning the 'higher strata' – in this case, Jewish labour – against its effects.[17] This is the economic function of the 'guest worker'. If Palestinian workers from the territories enjoy a peculiar status, it is only in that they have been made 'guests' in their own economy.

5

Palestinian Civil Society

On the eve of the installation of the Palestinian National Authority in July 1994, the only inkling Palestinians had of the political and legal nature of their imminent self-rule was the PLO Legal Committee's publication of three versions of its provisional constitution, known as the draft Basic Law for the National Authority in the Transitional Period.

The Basic Law is heavily circumscribed by the Oslo accords and even more so by the Cairo security agreement on Gaza and Jericho of 4 May 1994. Ostensibly it articulates the framework for Palestinian self-government. But under the DOP the only functions where the PNA has an unambiguous power to legislate are education, tourism, social welfare, health and direct taxation. Furthermore, this jurisdiction is personal rather than territorial, applying to Palestinians in the autonomy area but not to Israeli civilians, soldiers, settlers or corporations 'existing in' the autonomous enclaves. Israel retains sovereignty over all other policy areas, including, as affirmed by the Cairo agreement, the 2000 or so military orders issued during the occupation which remain in force during the interim period unless abrogated by the joint Israeli–Palestinian Legislative Sub-Committee.

The functioning of this sub-committee theoretically grants an Israeli veto over all Palestinian legislation, and Israeli supervision over the PNA's legislature and judiciary, including powers to 'approve' which Palestinians serve on it. The source of the Basic Law's authority thus derives not from the PNA, and still less the Palestinian people, but from Israel – a point rammed home by the legal adviser to Israel's Foreign Ministry, Joel Singer. The new Palestinian entity, he said in February 1994, 'will not be independent or sovereign in nature, but rather will be legally subordinate to the authority of the military government' in the territories.

Despite these limitations, the Basic Law is an important text. It serves as an 'aspirational document' which could lay the groundwork for an independent Palestinian future, albeit in an immediate context of limited self-government.[1] The legal and political arrangements the Basic Law envisages, as well as the interests and institutions it empowers, are likely to act as the basis for any definitive Palestinian constitution drawn up on completion of the five-year transitional period.

The Basic Law

The Basic Law stipulates no less than 39 fundamental rights and freedoms of the Palestinian people, and endorses adherence to various international covenants, including the Universal Declaration of Human Rights and the International Covenant on Civil and Political Rights. Yet these rights are embedded and anticipated within an extremely centralised form of self-government. Executive, legislative and judicial power is largely concentrated in the hands of the president of the Council of the National Authority (NAC). The president, who may also act as prime minister in a legislative council of ministers, has power of appointment over an 'independent' judiciary and is 'supreme commander' over the Palestinian security forces.

These powers are entrusted until the NAC can be popularly elected. But in contrast to the Basic Law's detail over the extent of presidential sway, it is dangerously vague over the content, authority and purpose of elections. Nowhere, for instance, is the obligation to provide for an electoral franchise protected. While the Basic Law refers to 'elected bodies', there is no definition of citizenship or qualifications to vote, and virtually no specification of offices to be controlled by democratic choice. Even the formation of political parties and right of assembly is subject to the PNA's approval of 'their objectives and activities'.

Even more problematic is the Basic Law's conceptualisation of the PLO as an extra-PNA body, yet one which commands absolute powers over it. The responsibility for establishing the NAC, appointing its members and detailing its powers resides with the PLO's Executive Council, not with the Palestine National Council, constitutionally the sovereign decision-making body of the PLO. The Basic Law also allows the president, 'as Chairman of the PLO Executive Committee', to exercise powers 'prescribed for him [sic] in the Basic Laws of the PLO, the resolutions of the PNC, the Central Council of the PLO and the Executive Committee of the PLO'. Thus even if the PNA manages to achieve some legal and democratic check over the centralising thrust of its presidency, the latter may still rule at will by invoking the extra-constitutional powers of the PLO.

The sum of the Basic Law's provisions, as one commentary puts it, amounts to the PLO's 'old Tunis-based regime in new constitutional garb'.[2] The hope of many Palestinians is that the centralism and bureaucratism of the Basic Law are likely to come in conflict with a relatively dynamic, pluralistic and progressive Palestinian civil society that has evolved via national and political struggle in the occupied territories, particularly during the intifada.

Palestinian NGOs

Palestinian civil society in the occupied territories is peculiar in one fundamental respect. It encompasses not only social organisations such as the family, mosques, churches, trade unions, media institutions, sports clubs and the like, but also a *de facto* political society based on Palestinian non-governmental organisations (NGOs). Forged around nationally-contested issues like agriculture, health, education, human rights and labour, these NGO's have historically comprised a counter-hegemonic, nationalist bloc against the occupation, 'an infrastructure of resistance' that not only developed in the absence of state structures but were politically defined by that absence.

Palestinian NGOs thus drew legitimacy not from actual state power in the territories – the Israeli military government – but from the 'surrogate power' afforded by the PLO and from national and community struggles generally. The existence of a PNA, a quasi-governmental structure, in Gaza and the West Bank has meant that these organisations not only have to sort out their novel political and legal relations with it, but also have to redefine and relocate their role in the national struggle.

Given these peculiarities, it was clear from the moment the DOP was signed that relations between the incoming PLO administration and the NGOs were going to be tense, with each staking out their respective turfs and articulating their historically different experiences and political visions. 'After Oslo – and even before – the PLO was trying to control the NGOs', said Umayya Khammash, a physician affiliated with the Union of Palestinian Medical Relief Committees (MRC). 'It understood that we had power in the occupied territories, both through our networks with international organisations and through our base in the community.'

This power is twofold. On the one hand, Palestinian NGOs run a formidable service provision infrastructure. According to MRC president Mustafa Barghouti, at the time of the Oslo signing NGOs operated 'about 60 per cent of primary health care services, 100 per cent of pre-school services, 100 per cent of disability rehabilitation services and 30 per cent of the educational network in the West Bank and Gaza'.[3] Organisations like the medical and agricultural relief committees, and women's and human rights groups, have been bastions of Palestinian independents and the PLO left, reflecting Fatah's historical neglect towards developing community-based organisations inside the territories. The upshot was an initial NGO stance towards the DOP that ranged from critical to hostile, and in all cases deeply suspicious of the PLO's centralising and coopting overtures.

In the run-up to Oslo, the PLO established a number of Higher Councils with responsibility for public services such as health, housing and education. Initially these were viewed as prototypes for the ministries of the nascent PNA. After the ministries were established, however, the Higher Councils continued to function, creating a fog between their role and that of the PNA's departments.

In the summer of 1993 and again in June 1994, the PLO 'outside' circulated a letter to all international organisations and foreign governments explaining that the Higher Councils would remain the 'party responsible' for 'all international relations ... on behalf of the Palestinian people', including all financial transactions. When pressed to clarify what this meant, the Health Council's 'coordinator' of NGOs, Dr Yusif Awadallah, said that under self-rule the Higher Councils would 'represent the interests of both the Authority and the NGOs'.[4]

Many NGOs saw this attempt to 'represent' them as a ploy to marginalise their influence and tap into their sources of foreign funds. This was not paranoia. The year after Oslo witnessed a collapse of NGO-run services, as foreign funders diverted aid to the PNA's fledgeling ministries. But, lacking any public infrastructure, or expertise to run it, the PNA's takeover of services often resulted in their abandonment, particularly in the territories' poorer regions. 'During the past year alone', said Barghouti, '66 per cent of the rural clinics in the most deprived area of the West Bank – the Jenin district – have closed due to lack of money.'[5]

In October 1993, representatives of some 20 NGOs met in Ramallah. They drew up a position paper outlining the 'key principles' which they felt should govern the NGOs future relations with the PNA. The statement was subsequently endorsed by 60 Palestinian NGOs.

NGOs, the paper argues, must preserve their 'total independence' from the PNA's structures and institutions, and the right to 'maintain their existing relations of cooperation, and to form new ones, with international agencies ...'. Further, NGOs, and particularly human rights bodies, must be allowed to 'continuously observe' PNA activity, insisting that this be in harmony with 'democratic values'. They will also continue to lobby for and defend the rights of deprived social sectors, 'especially women, children and the disabled' and 'mobilise community resources for action'. Finally, given the changed conditions of self-rule, NGOs must embark on 'a comprehensive evaluation of their activities', ensuring that they are run according to the principles of 'professionalism, democracy and public accountability'.

With the exception of the last point, the paper is essentially defensive in tone: NGOs organising to defend what they have. Yet the reality of the PNA has forced NGOs to review critically both their conceptualisation and strategies for Palestinian civil society.

For Mustafa Barghouti, this entails the NGOs taking a proactive stance vis-à-vis the PNA, not only a defensive one. The components of a positive relation with the PNA, he said, would involve not merely clear separation and monitoring, but also that NGOs share in strategy formulation with the PNA, plan service provision for the interim period, and participate in coordinating structures to ensure 'cooperation in a democratic manner'. NGOs should also act to generate 'developmental models' for the PNA based on the specific conditions and needs of Palestinian society.[6]

Whether the PNA will buy into this notion of a 'developmental contract' with the NGOs remains to be seen. It appears so far that while the NGOs seek 'coordination *with* the PNA', the authority seeks coordination *over* them. In September 1994, the PNA's Ministry of Justice issued a press statement calling on all local and foreign NGOs operating under its jurisdiction to register their organisations. The motive behind this, said Jamal Zaqout of the PNA/Israeli Liaison Committee on Civil Affairs, was entirely benign:

> There are two purposes behind registration. Firstly, to transfer the relation that existed between the NGOs and the occupation author-ities to one that should now exist between the NGOs and the PNA. Secondly, the PNA has the right to know if NGOs are functioning correctly or not. Through registration, the PNA can tell them to organise their affairs properly.[7]

Umayya Khammash, however, is less sanguine about the implications of registration:

> The motive behind registration is control. We agree that there must be a legal framework between the PNA and the NGOs, a regulated relationship. But this has to evolve out of dialogue and be structured by the Palestinian NGO experience inside the territories. It cannot be imposed from above.[8]

In October 1994, the NGO coalition publicly refused to register with the PNA. Without a clear legal basis, they argued, registration was an information-gathering exercise that did not require 'permission' from the PNA. Instead, the coalition proposed that every existing NGO should be registered automatically until a clear 'legal-constitutional framework' governing their relations with the PNA is established. To this end, it has opened a dialogue with the Palestinian Economic Council for Development and Reconstruction (PECDAR) aimed at identifying these relations and focusing on the legal rights of NGOs under the PNA.

A further problem for the NGOs is the likely legal basis of this 'coordination'. The NGOs cannot submit to any legal incorporation by the PNA if these laws are derived from the Oslo and Cairo security agreements. Mustafa Barghouti said: 'We are entering a new era with new requirements, but we are still operating out of the previous one ... The PNA remains under Israel's direction, economically and politically.'[9]

For Barghouti, it is important to remember that

Israel developed its infrastructure successfully through popular, civil and semi-governmental organisations. It was built from the bottom to the top. The only outlet allowed now for the Palestinians is the reinforcement and initiation of various kinds of popular, public and developmental organisations and groups. The real commitment to peace necessitates ignoring the [Oslo and Cairo] agreements and building an unshakeable front on the basis of the Palestinian national aims.[10]

One obstacle, of course, is that the Israelis will view such nationalist attempts at state-building as violations of the DOP and will lean on the PNA to put a stop to them. Given Israel's military muscle on the one hand and the leverage it can mobilise via the donors on the other, the stage would then be set for some kind of stand-off between the PNA and the 'popular and civil organisations'. Whether the NGOs would be strong enough as a sector to resist these combined pressures is an open but doubtful proposition. 'Palestinian and non-Palestinian NGOs have an important role to play in the coming period', said Palestinian political scientist George Giacaman, but,

the strength of civil society in terms of its ability to limit government authority and influence policy derives from the existence of a vibrant and dynamic political opposition .... Without an organised political opposition struggling to keep at bay government encroachment upon society, the work of the NGOs can easily be curtailed, restricted and marginalised by legal and extra-legal means.[11]

The Opposition

The crisis of representation that Oslo prompted within Fatah in the territories was felt no less among the PLO opposition, particularly in the Popular and Democratic Fronts for the Liberation of Palestine (PFLP and DFLP). They, too, were constricted by an organisational structure and ideology unable to come to grips with the new political realities thrown up by self-rule. Since Oslo, opposition politics has been marked by theoretical poverty and organisational paralysis.

The PFLP and DFLP's immediate response to Oslo was to resign from all PLO bodies and form a rejectionist bloc, along with Hamas and Islamic Jihad and a medley of Arab satellite organisations. Threatening to use 'all means necessary' to abort the agreement, the rejectionists instead became bogged down in organisational wrangles. Hamas demanded, 'as the largest opposition force', 40 per cent representation on all 'joint' committees, while the PLO factions called for equal shares. The matter was formally resolved in the secularists' favour in January 1994 with the formation of the Palestinian Forces Alliance (PFA).

As soon as the alliance had surmounted the representational quarrel, it foundered on the utter incompatibility of its constituents' political aims. The main plank of the PFLP and DFLP was reform of the PLO and removal of the 'liquidationist' Arafat leadership. Hamas was more ambivalent about the fate of the PLO and refused, for the time being, to work under its umbrella. Similarly, while the PLO opposition argued that the question of Palestine must be grounded on international law (specifically the implementation of UN Resolutions 242 and 338), Hamas had long held the view that any UN partition plan 'was no more legitimate than the borders of Gaza and Jericho'.[12]

Most observers regarded this attempt to build a national-Islamist bloc as doomed from the outset. The prognosis has been borne out. By April 1994, Popular Front leader Abu Ali Mustafa complained that there was 'no field organisation' between the PLO opposition and Hamas in the territories. In July 1994, Gaza PFLP activist Ghazi Abu Jiab stated bluntly that the 'alliance between us and Hamas has proved a failure and is now over'.[13]

The damage, however, had been done. In the months immediately after Oslo, the PLO opposition, hamstrung by its coalition with the Islamists, mounted not a single independent mobilisation against the agreement. Rather, it was Hamas or the pro-Oslo Fatah and Fida factions which, on the ground, initiated mass actions around the contested issues of prisoners, settlements and Jerusalem as a means of putting pressure on the PLO delegation.

Whenever the PLO opposition was provoked into action, it tended to be reactive. In the aftermath of the Hebron massacre – perhaps the greatest opportunity for the opposition to reformulate, at least the terms of the DOP – the PFLP and DFLP united temporarily with Fatah activists to revive the United National Leadership (UNL). But the conditions of the UNL's previous success – the intifada – no longer held. What now dominated the political landscape was Oslo, and a PLO fractured by it. The reformed UNL issued one leaflet condemning the massacre and then, predictably, disappeared.

Even more culpably, the PLO opposition had yet to formulate a coherent political programme outlining its positions vis-à-vis the Palestinian self-government. When pressed to construct a positive political alternative to Oslo, the opposition's official line was that 'it is not our job to create a new alternative, but to guard the original agenda of the PLO, which the PLO relinquished in the agreement'.[14] This may have been politically correct on a scale of orthodoxy: it was disastrous on the terrain of real politics. One year after Oslo, opinion polls in the territories registered the combined support for the PLO opposition to be less than 10 per cent.

With the installation of the Palestinian Authority, there were signs of a pragmatic shift. In June 1994, veteran PFLP leader George Habash called on the opposition 'not to take a negative stance towards Palestinian institutions that offer services during the interim phase and to develop its ... social and national performance in a way that serves its policies'.[15] Inside the territories, figures like Abu Jiab have increasingly spoken of the opposition's current priorities being not just to confront the agreement, but equally to prevent Arafat from establishing 'a dictatorial self-rule'.

There has also been dissension over future relations between the opposition organisations inside the territories and in the diaspora, a debate that is bound to intensify as PFLP and DFLP cadres return to Palestine. Many 'inside' activists argue that the preponderance of the Damascus-based leadership in decision-making is at the root of the opposition's baneful performance since Oslo, as the outside 'appropriates authority from institutions' within and 'disciplines them for the role of relaying orders to the rank and file'.[16]

This bureaucratic conception of politics, said Abu Jiab, also accounts for the PLO opposition's historic failure to capitalise on the gains of the intifada when compared to the Islamists' relative success. 'Hamas' growth in the uprising can be attributed to the fact that it has one, and only one, leadership – inside', he said, 'and therefore does not suffer from the results of having a variety of leadership groups, or of the existence of various centres which issue their directives from a distance, without being directly or strongly connected to what is going on here'.[17]

If the PLO opposition is to avoid the very real charge of irrelevance and meet the challenges of the interim period, it will have to reform its organisational structure and adapt its short-term political aims. 'Everything suggests that the time has come to move from the present system of factions to a system of political parties with all that entails', said former DFLP member Jamil Hilal, 'including making them accountable to the public, making known their political and social programmes, and instituting a system of democratic competition for positions of public responsibility and office'.[18]

Such a posture need not preclude underground forms of organisation, but it would establish the opposition's primary role for the interim period as a political one, laying the foundations of a democratic Palestinian civil society. 'The opposition will be unable to stay alive except under a PNA that guarantees freedom of association and political activity, defends civil liberties, allows public decision-making and governs by rule of law instead of the random rule of individual or party', said George Giacaman. In short, 'the pillar of Palestinian civil society is going to be the presence of opposition parties'.[19]

A second step would be for the opposition to lend its political weight to those demanding democratic reform of the PLO, particularly the Palestinian independents, the Palestine People's Party and numerous Fatah dissidents. Yet for this alliance to be meaningful it would not only have to go beyond the now wholly sterile debate as to whether one is for or against Oslo; it would have to agree on an overhaul of the old quota system, whereby PLO factions gained automatic representation on bodies like the PNC, in favour of a democratic system based on direct elections both inside and outside the territories. In other words, it would mean the opposition forswearing the very mechanism that has ensured its presence on PLO bodies for the last 25 years.

Finally, the process of going public should necessitate a rigorous and open debate within the opposition about its whole national programme, and especially its allegiance to old-style Marxist-Leninism and its paucity of any kind of social policy. If 'no ideology but nationalism' was historically a hallmark of Fatah, the period since Oslo – and even before – has starkly exposed the opposition's equivalent poverty on cultural matters, especially when confronted by the clear, if reactionary, social visions offered by Hamas.

The Palestinian Women's Movement

The Palestinian women's movement assumed its modern form in the early 1980s. Born out of nationalist and grassroots activism, the movement's vanguard were the women's committees allied to the PLO's four main factions. The intifada rendered these women politically visible, as women's committees played a crucial role in mobilising women for demonstrations, marches and sit-ins. Women were also the backbone of many popular committees set up to provide alternative services in agriculture, education, food storage and health.[20]

Yet, as many Palestinian women activists concede, the experience has not registered any lasting qualitative changes in women's political, social or economic power. For activist Islah Jad, this lack of change stems from the movement's ongoing political dependence on the PLO factions: 'There has been no gender agenda for the women's movement until now', she said. 'Women's political participation remains dependent on development – positive or negative – at the level of the leadership', a leadership which historically has consigned women's activism to 'social service work with a political connotation'.[21]

It is this absence of a social critique in Palestinian nationalism that a handful of women intellectuals and factions from the women's committees sought to redress in the wake of Oslo. For them, the priorities facing the movement under self-rule are less the occupation than civic issues around future legislation, the forthcoming PNA elections and the need to curb the rising cultural influence of Hamas.

In October 1993, the Technical Committee – a women's advisory body set up by the PLO after the Madrid Conference – embarked on an electoral education campaign among women in the territories, explaining rights and procedures for voting. The import of the campaign was not merely instrumental, but political and politicising. 'We didn't want women to vote according to political affiliation', Jad says,

> because as yet none of the PLO factions have anything to offer women. Rather, we wanted to educate women to judge the factions on the basis of their political and social policies for women. The role of the women's committees was to impress on their leaderships the electoral importance of these issues, since women comprise 54 per cent of the Palestinian electorate.[22]

This attempt to forgo factionalism, however, quickly fell victim to it. Women belonging to those PLO factions opposed to Oslo saw the 'electoral education campaign' as simply a political ruse to drum up support for the DOP and the Fatah-dominated PLO leadership. 'Should we fight for the adoption of women's rights by the self-government institutions which were themselves undemocratically appointed?', asks Suha Barghouti of the PFLP-aligned Palestinian Women's Committees. 'I do not believe our activities should be directed to the PNA.'[23]

To avoid these dissensions, the struggle for women's legal rights in the autonomy was quietly removed from the auspices of the Technical Committee. In its stead emerged an ad hoc, politically independent 'Document Committee', so called because its aim was to produce a paper detailing a women's 'Bill of Rights'. The campaign had the blessing of PLO's General Union of Palestinian Women and the PLO opposition alike. The document, finally published in August 1994, argues for an essentially egalitarian and secularist vision of women's legal rights in employment, education, health and crime. It is tellingly circumspect, though, on the crucial issues of family law and personal status. This is due to internal and as yet unresolved debates within the women's movement as to the correct posture vis-à-vis the Islamists' social agenda: outright confrontation on the grounds of religious pluralism, or 'acts of accommodating protest'.

For many Palestinian women activists, the threat of an emergent Islamist culture is the worst-case scenario for self-rule. Yet, as Islah Jad admits, it is a real prospect. The danger for women's rights lies not so much in the ambition of Hamas's social demands, she said, but in their calculated moderation. Many mainstream nationalist men would find little to object to in Hamas's call that *shari'a* remain the basis of all personal law in the territories, or even with the Islamists' codification of women's primary role as that of 'mother and producer of Muslims'.

There are already clear signs that Hamas's gradualism is paying off. After Oslo, discussions were held between the PLO's Education Department in Tunis and the Union of Islamic Scholars in the occupied territories to 'evaluate' the ideological content of a future Palestinian school curriculum.[24] And Jad detects an Islamist influence in the drafts of the Basic Law through their 'significant silences' on the matter of women's rights. 'In the first draft of the Basic Law submitted by the PNC's Legal Committee', she said,

> there was no statement affirming equality between men and women. When women made a fuss, the Committee's Chair, Anis al-Qasim, said it was an oversight. When the second draft was submitted, it referred to all international agreements governing

human rights except the 1979 UN agreement outlawing all forms of discrimination against women.[25]

The reason for this omission, said Jad, was less error than political prudence.

Qasim told us that such a pledge would contradict local – that is *shari'a* – law. He said the incoming PNA was going to be weak and was not going to open up unnecessary battles. His meaning was crystal clear: if Palestinian women wanted to secure their rights, they would have to go out in the field and flex their muscles.[26]

The 'field' is Palestinian civil society and activists in the women's movement have been debating responses. For Palestinian lawyer Hanan Bakri, to centre women's social struggle on a blanket acceptance or rejection of *shari'a* is to lose it. 'Since most of our society is religious and conservative', she said, 'we should use the opportunities in Islam to try and interpret existing laws in a way that is more appropriate to the present age'.[27]

Other women argue for a more assertive and secularist defence of women rights. Women, they say, must define an agenda of basic rights and laws that commands the support of all women's groups, regardless of factional allegiance, and build a lobby to activate women's electoral strength when voting happens. For Palestinian feminist Rita Giacaman, 'a truly independent agenda' requires that 'Palestinian women set about forging alliances with other oppressed groups around issues of democracy and equality'.[28]

One problem is the dependability of the allies. The most natural coalition for any genuinely independent women's movement would be the 'nationalist' NGOs. Many of these, however, are the preserve of the PLO left. The question is whether women in these organisations are willing or able to forge a gender policy independent of their factional leadership's opposition to Oslo. For PFLP activists like Suha Barghouti, it is a moot point which constitutes the gravest threat – the social agenda of Hamas or the political agenda of the incoming authority. 'Support or opposition to the DOP has become the defining factor', she said. 'It is impossible to divide the larger political situation from the women's question.'[29]

The upshot of analyses like these has been the uncomfortable and not very effective political alliance between leftist organisations and the Islamists, based on their mutual opposition to the PNA. 'It is a dangerous alliance', admits one PFLP woman activist, 'but it is legitimate because the main aim is to do away with self-government.

It is bringing to us a very undemocratic, fascist regime. The alliance, moreover, is only political, and does not touch on our social programme.'[30]
This is a strategy fraught with perils. If it 'does not touch' on social issues, this is only because, in the name of a national-Islamic unity, it suppresses any debate about them. It therefore threatens to repeat the cardinal error that the UNL, including its leftist factions, made in the intifada. Then, argues Giacaman, the nationalists conceded much of the cultural ground to Hamas because they 'could only conceive of the Islamists in narrowly factional terms, and not as a social force in Palestinian society at large'.[31]
Islah Jad agrees. While the days when Palestinian women would grant unthinking fidelity to the PLO 'are over for good', she nonetheless advocates a policy of conditional support vis-à-vis the PNA. It is a 'foot in/foot out' strategy, where women consolidate their independent organisations at the grassroots but continue to lobby for a position and a voice in the emerging authority.[32] 'If women don't utilise the space that autonomy affords to pursue their own independent agenda', she said, 'if we focus exclusively on the narrow political question as to whether we're for or against the PNA, then in effect we are giving the social and legal terrain to Hamas. And if we do that, we are finished.'[33]

Trade Unions

By far the strongest potential sector of civil society in the occupied territories is the Palestinian working class. According to the Democracy and Workers' Rights Centre in Ramallah, at the time of Israel's closure of the territories in April 1993 the Palestinian labour force consisted of 339,000 workers, with 90,000 working in the West Bank, 60,000 in Gaza, and a colossal 189,000 working inside Israel.
Yet in the run-up to Oslo the political influence of this potentially crucial economic muscle was almost wholly debilitated, for three reasons. After 27 years of Israeli occupation, and especially the chronic dependency of the territories' economy on the Israeli economy that this had engendered, Palestinian workers constituted, in the opinion of one analyst, 'a nascent migrant-worker class of predominantly nationalist orientation'.[34] The typical nature of their work in both Israel and the territories was casual, informal, unskilled and itinerant, with all the attendant problems for trade union organisation that such a workforce entailed. By dint of this situation, Palestinian workers viewed their main adversary as less their own bourgeoisie than the military occupation. When they did take collective action,

as during the intifada, class demands were subordinate to national-ist demands. The upshot was an extremely low level of trade union consciousness.

Second, by the time of the Oslo agreement, Palestinian workers were still reeling from a massive blow to their jobs and livelihoods. From April 1993 onwards, the Israelis repeatedly closed the territories, not just as a temporary punishment for Palestinian 'security' offences but also as a vehicle for physically separating Gaza and the West Bank from the Israeli economy and from each other, and to whittle down the number of Palestinian workers inside the Green Line. By October 1994, Israel had imported 53,000 foreign workers from southeast Asia and Eastern Europe to do the jobs Palestinians once did. By late 1993, on any one day no more than 60,000 Palestinians from the West Bank and Gaza were working in Israel. The results were unemployment rates of 25 per cent across the territories as a whole and 52 per cent in Gaza, reducing income earned in Israel from $920 million in 1992 to $400 million in 1994.[35]

Finally, Palestinian trade unions were internally divided along factional lines. Prior to Oslo, there were no fewer than three 'general' trade union federations operating in the territories: a Fatah-controlled federation in Gaza and two federations in the West Bank, one aligned with the DFLP and the other a bloc of Fatah, People's Party and PFLP-controlled unions.

Riven by political disputes such as the Madrid peace process, the federations competed with each other for members, power and turf. The result was an upsurge of factional unions across the territories in inverse ratio to their influence among Palestinian workers. By the summer of 1993, there were 161 'political' unions in the West Bank and Gaza, but with a combined membership of not more than 6000 workers, most of whom were politically affiliated.[36]

Such factionalism not only did nothing to defend workers' interests; it actively inhibited the development of trade union values and organisation. The 'artificial unity' of the PLO factions 'did not improve the unions' work, nor did it reinforce its [sic] relations with workers', said Mustafa Barghouti. 'On the contrary, the union movement regressed like never before, because none of the leaders were interested in their own union's constituency.'[37]

The existence of the DOP did impose a degree of realism on Pales-tinian trade unions, though without challenging their factional basis. In October 1993, the three federations agreed to unify their ranks on the condition that general elections would be held for a new executive by March 1995. In the meantime, the federations would be 'internally reorganised' on a district rather than factional basis.

No sooner had the federations kicked off the unification process 'inside', however, than it was stymied by the intervention of the PLO's Tunis-based General Union of Palestinian Workers. In the opinion of its general secretary, Haidar Ibrahim, the new situation created by Oslo called for the immediate amalgamation of the two wings of the Palestinian trade union movement. This 'fusion' was to be heavily slanted in favour of Tunis. Of the General Union's 19-seat executive, only two places were allocated for union representatives from inside the territories: one for Gaza federation leader Rasem Bayari and the other for West Bank head Shaher Said.[38]

This preponderance of the outside over inside proved baneful, especially in what was perhaps the Palestinian trade unions' most important immediate challenge – its negotiations with the Israeli trade union federation, the Histadrut. Under the Paris protocol, 75 per cent of all Palestinian workers' tax and welfare deductions paid to Israel are to be disbursed to the PNA. Of these deductions, about 1 per cent is for union dues. A dispute between Israeli and Palestinian negotiators quickly arose, however, as to when the monies owed were to be backdated. The Palestinian position was that payment was retroactive to October 1970, when Israel labour exchanges started to register Palestinians to work in Israel. In the 24 years since, around 700,000 Palestinian workers legally worked in Israeli, and paid Israeli taxes, but received only scant services. This would bring the estimated amount owed by Israel to the PNA to between $1.5 and $3 billion.[39] The Israelis argued that backpay should be from the signing of the DOP, since before that workers' deductions were used to pay for Israeli government 'services'.

As regards union fees, the Histadrut argued that a percentage, backdated to the signing of the DOP, should go to the federations in the West Bank and Gaza while the Histradut should continue to hold a percentage, since the Paris accord allows both Israeli and Palestinian unions to organise in each other's economies. In the meantime, the Histadrut would transfer New Israeli Shekels (NIS) 3 million to Palestinian trade unions 'up front'. Not surprisingly, both the Gaza and West Bank federations flatly refused the deal.

At this point the PLO's General Union, in the person of Arafat himself, stepped in. In September 1994 discussions with Histadrut representatives, Arafat agreed to defer negotiations on the backpay issue for one year, on the condition that the Israeli union upped the advance payment from NIS 3 million to NIS 8 million. In return, the Histadrut proposal on 'equal shares' between itself and the Palestinian federations would hold until the resumption of the backpay talks.

These manoeuvres suggest that the future of Palestinian trade unions is likely to be as plagued by factionalism as its past, only now the PNA will have the augmented role of labour enforcement agency. The challenge facing the Palestinian workers' movement is clear. 'Our cardinal role is to democratise the unions to put them on an independent footing', said the director of the Democracy and Workers' Rights Centre, Hassan Barghouti.

The current factional leadership will then face a choice: either resign or be held accountable to their membership by fighting on labour issues rather than narrowly factional issues. I'm not just talking about Fatah here. All of the PLO factions have the same abusive attitude to trade unions, using them as mere fronts for their political line.[40]

If Palestinian trade unions can achieve political independence, Barghouti believes, there are opportunities for Palestinian workers during the interim period, even in their unequal relations with the Histadrut. 'One of the good things about the new relationship with the Histadrut is that it will force Palestinian trade unions to organise around trade union issues', he said. 'Whatever the limitations of the Paris agreement, it permits recruitment. And if Palestinian trade unions don't fight to recruit workers in Israel and the territories, the Histadrut will.'

The greatest challenge facing any nascent union movement in the autonomy is likely to be the staking out of an independent position with the PNA. 'In the draft Basic Law', Barghouti explains,

it states that Palestinian workers can be paid in wages or in goods. This is a clear violation of every international labour law. So in whose interest is this clause? Clearly, the old Palestinian landowning class who still use payment in kind for their employees.[41]

It is already clear, says Barghouti, that the PNA is likely to be disproportionately representative of Palestine's capitalist class. 'More than 50 per cent of Arafat's appointed ministers are either landowners or employers', he says.

Given the class composition of the PNA and economic scenarios for self-rule anticipated by the Paris agreement, Palestinian workers are likely to pay a high price for autonomy. By the same token, they also have the greatest interest in resisting it. In Barghouti's opinion, this resistance cannot be channelled along 'classic class struggle forms'. Rather, Palestinian workers must become the leading force in a broad democratic coalition made up of Palestinian NGOs, the women's movement and political parties to chart an independent future for self-rule in opposition to both the dictates of Israel and the PNA's probable complicity with it. 'Palestinian trade unions cannot be simply self-interested or oppositional in their attitude to the PNA', Barghouti says.

In the interim period, our terrain is not going to be confined solely to economic issues; it will also cover law, democracy, human rights, social provision and education – in short, development. The next stage requires a new kind of struggle in which workers should take increasing responsibility for the welfare of the Palestinian nation.[42]

6

Arafat's Rule: The Debut of the Palestinian Authority

On 1 July 1994, Arafat set foot on Palestinian soil for the first time in 27 years. Palestinians in Gaza and Jericho turned out in the thousands rather than hundreds of thousands to greet him, not just because the previous nine months had shown how heavily the deck was still stacked against them, but also because they were aware of the monumental risks to their national aspiration of self-determination. 'Getting rid of the Israelis was hard', said one Gazan at the time, 'but not compared to building a state'.

Arafat himself drew attention to these realities. Gaza and Jericho were 'the first steps' to Palestinian control over the entire occupied territories, he asserted. 'There will be hardship, there will be hunger and, as always, Palestinians must rely on no one but themselves', he told a crowd at Gaza's Jabalya refugee camp.

Palestinians appreciated Arafat's honesty, though most had bought into Oslo in the belief that it would alleviate rather than augment their deprivation. They were also worried by their first experiences with the PLO-Tunis in charge, and particularly its 'culture of security'.[1] Arafat's return had been preceded by the arrival of a 7000-strong Palestinian police force, actually units of the PLO's Palestinian Liberation Army (PLA) decanted from different Arab states. Their sudden and overwhelming presence in the streets of Gaza and Jericho, coupled with a 125-member personal guard that accompanied the 'President' everywhere, left many 'insiders' apprehensive. 'The whole thing smacks of existing Arab governments', said Gaza community activist Ahmed Abdallah. 'Palestinians have suffered more than most from the absence of democracy in Arab society.'

No sooner had Arafat arrived than he chaired numerous PLO meetings, pronouncing on everything from the minutiae of Gaza's sewerage system to the future of the Palestinian women's movement. It was good public relations: one local Fatah leader claimed to be relieved that 'Arafat knew everything' and was firmly 'in control'. But it alarmed other Palestinians for whom such centralisation of power was at odds with the needs of a national movement that now had to transform itself into a polity for forging a state. 'Of course, I welcome Arafat's return', said Haidar Abd al-Shafi, but he conditioned his own participation in the nascent PNA on Arafat's 'broadening the base of PLO decision-making'. The weeks ahead saw the PLO leader largely disenfranchise the local Palestinian leadership, arrogating power either to himself or to PLO functionaries who had followed him from Tunis to Gaza and Jericho.

These themes – security, democracy, economic hardship – were to plague Arafat during the first six months of his rule. The worst of them was the Palestinians' dire economic situation. Arafat returned to a Gaza Strip with unemployment levels of around 50 per cent and an infrastructure virtually destroyed after 27 years of deliberate Israeli neglect. The delay in setting up the PNA and Israel's punitive closure policies aggravated the situation as did a six-month imbroglio between the PLO leader and the international donors who had pledged to underwrite the autonomy. The PLO had stood firm, Arafat told audiences in Gaza and Jericho, because Palestinians 'did not get rid of military occupation to fall under economic occupation'.

Economic Deconstruction

In October 1993, at a conference held under the auspices of the World Bank, 22 donor countries along with other regional and UN agencies pledged $2.1 billion to the Palestinian autonomy for the five-year interim period. If the aid was less than that required by the PLO's own estimate – which placed Palestinian 'developmental needs' at $11 billion over a seven-year period – it was nevertheless welcomed by Palestinian economists.[2] The donors' emphasis on funding 'a basic social and physical infrastructure', coupled with a thriving private sector 'as the main engine of growth', argued World Bank adviser Abdallah Bouhabib, was the only way to avoid creating 'an aid-dependent economy'.[3]

Yet no sooner had the pledges been made than they ran into a political minefield. In the absence of any Palestinian governmental structure in the West Bank and Gaza, the World Bank established the Palestinian Economic Council for Development and Reconstruction (PECDAR), whose remit was to implement 'immediate-impact projects', improving road, electricity and water services in the territories. These were labour-intensive projects, politically targeted for Palestinians 'to see very early that their situation will improve because of peace'.[4]

The problem was that PECDAR was answerable to the World Bank rather than to any 'national' Palestinian body. Arafat viewed this arrangement as a manoeuvre to circumvent his authority. In November 1993, he issued a decree stating that PECDAR would be accountable to the PNA president (himself) and that he would be its chairman. 'Arafat', said one UN official, 'has made himself accountable to Arafat.'

PECDAR's Managing Director, Yusuf Sayigh, immediately resigned on the grounds that the Council's 'responsibilities were being tied to political figureheads'. A group of diaspora Palestinian business-men submitted a memorandum to Arafat urging him to forgo the 'revolution mentality' of national liberation in favour of a 'state building mentality', in which institutions like PECDAR would enjoy independent decision-making powers and possess clear by-laws.[5] The memo was worded in a spirit of 'patriotic duty', but the message was clear: either Arafat must set about creating an autonomy with 'transparent' laws and regulations, or Palestinian private investment would not be forthcoming.

To no avail. In the run-up to the PNA's installation in July 1994, Arafat actively worked to disempower PECDAR, preferring to let the 'immediate-impact projects' stall until he and his administration were in Gaza and Jericho. 'For months we've been urging our leadership to put the necessary people in place', said PECDAR Policy Director Samir Abdallah, in June 1994. 'They did nothing about it.' The delay in aid, therefore, 'can't be blamed on anyone but ourselves'.

By the time Arafat returned, only about $60 million out of $570 million pledged for the first year of autonomy had been disbursed. Such a negligible amount made little difference to the 'quality of life' in the territories, and its economic impact had been wiped out by less favourable 'dividends' of the peace deal. As a result of the Paris agreement, for example, Palestinian agricultural produce had been granted relatively free export to the Israeli market, creating a 250 per cent hike in vegetable prices. Gaza also reeled from an Israeli inflation rate of 12 to 14 per cent.

On 17 July 1994, major confrontations between Palestinian workers and the IDF broke out at the Eretz checkpoint, Gaza's main artery into Israel, leaving two Palestinians dead and 75 injured. The Israeli government cast round for causes. The riots had been 'orchestrated by Hamas activists' bent on wrecking the peace agreement, said officials, and was also the fault of the Palestinian police who had not properly 'coordinated' with the IDF. For Palestinians, the reason was more banal and far more incendiary. 'Today's battle was a battle for a loaf of bread', said PNA Justice Minister Frieh Abu Midain. 'It was not premeditated by us or by the Israelis'.[6]

If the Eretz unrest alarmed the donors, it did not resolve the root cause of their dispute with Arafat. This was not about whether economic reconstruction should be in hands of Palestinian 'technocrats' like Sayigh or Abdallah, or politicians like Arafat. It had more to do with how and where the money was spent. Donors wanted aid tied to clear infrastructural projects; Arafat wanted it cashed into 'operational funds' to enable him to set up and finance his nascent administration.

By far the largest PNA 'operating cost' was the burgeoning security forces. The Cairo agreement had set a ceiling of 9000 police officers for Gaza and Jericho, but by December 1994 the payroll had grown to over 13,000 personnel, largely due to Arafat's expansion of his multiple 'preventive security' intelligence agencies. If Arafat needed a police force of this size, the donors argued, it would have to be covered by the PNA's own revenues.

Due to a mix of Israeli obstruction in handing over accurate tax records and the PNA's own failure at setting up a workable tax structure, revenues generated out of the PNA's initial direct taxation amounted to no more than $3 million a month. The bill for police salaries alone came to $4.2 million a month, excluding other expenditures such as education, health and social welfare. Under such circumstances, said Rabin, Israel would not transfer these 'early empowerment' services until the PNA established 'a real financial arrangement' with the donors.

In an attempt to break the impasse, the UN appointed Terje Larsen, the Norwegian social scientist who, as its Special Coordinator, served as 'midwife' to the Oslo accords. Under the compromise he brokered, donors could fund large-scale infrastructural projects through PECDAR, while for medium and small labour-intensive projects a UN umbrella body would act as a 'bridging mechanism' for the PNA. 'So donors put the money in the UN account and it goes to the PNA's account the next day, and we monitor projects', said Larsen. These 'projects' would include schemes designed to chip away at Gaza's chronic unemployment levels; they would also cover 'arrangements' whereby individual donor countries could pay for the upkeep of the Palestinian police.

At a special donor conference in Brussels in November 1994, Arafat, with the active support of the UN and the Israelis, scored a partial victory in his year-long tussle with the World Bank. The donor countries agreed to release $102 million to underwrite the PNA's projected $123 million budget deficit for 1994, and $23 million for a crash public works programme to create 5000 jobs in Gaza. Since the main money was marked almost wholly for operational expenses – including police salaries – Rabin's 'real financial arrangement' had been secured. Israel transferred the 'early empowerment' services of health, social welfare, education, tourism and direct taxation to Palestinian control. For Larsen, Brussels signalled a victory of political pragmatism over economic ambition. 'The donor effort has been a failure', he had said in November. 'There has been an over-emphasis on long-term projects, but the poor and hungry and sick can't wait. If there is no food for the children and no heat for the winter, who will support the PNA and the peace process?'[7]

Many Palestinian economists and professionals, however, were dismayed by Brussels. They had earlier voiced the belief that the World Bank and other international agencies would somehow impose on the PLO a more collegial and rational approach to economic decision-making.[8] This vision crumbled as each institution gradually bought into Israel's (and increasingly Arafat's) security-led vision of the self-rule. A 13,000-strong police force would constitute a massive and permanent drain on the PNA's locally generated revenue, and send the worst possible message to potential investors in the autonomy. Any authority that required more police officers than schoolteachers commanded little legitimacy and anticipated major public resistance to its policies. Neither scenario is particularly good for business. Israel's acquiescence to such a massive Palestinian security force on its doorstep, said PPP leader Bashir Barghouti, could only mean that the PNA would be 'an instrument in the hands of the Israeli authorities, executing what Israel sees fit for its security'.[9]

Preventive Security

The issue of 'a strong Palestinian police force' had dominated the PLO/Israeli negotiations, especially following the Hebron massacre. After initial hesitation, the Israelis consented to a 9000-person force, 7000 of whom would be recruited from PLA units based in Egypt, Jordan, Sudan, Yemen, Iraq and Algeria. The Israelis and the PLO also agreed that the police's commanders should be 'outsiders' like PLA Colonel Nasir Yusuf and General Ghazi Jabali, since they were considered more loyal to Arafat and less hostile to the occupation than 'inside' Palestinians.

Formally, the police comprised four divisions: a civil defence force responsible for crime and traffic, recruited largely from inside the territories; a national guard responsible for 'joint security' with the IDF, made up of PLA battalions; an emergency force responsible for 'public order'; and an intelligence service to monitor 'internal Palestinian security'. But the chief duty of these forces overall was to ensure the implementation of the security provisions of the Cairo agreement. Thus, while the police's powers vis-à-vis Israelis in the autonomy are extremely limited – able to check Israeli vehicles, for instance, but unable to stop Israeli military personnel – their remit vis-à-vis Palestinians is both sweeping and wholly vague, empowering them to 'take all measures necessary to prevent hostile acts ... against Israeli settlements, infrastructure and military installations'.

The crucial police division is intelligence, or the Preventive Security Apparatus (PSA). This is led and staffed by 'inside' Palestinians, wholly recruited from Arafat's Fatah movement and particularly its armed wing, the Fatah Hawks. By appointing Fatah leaders with a history of national struggle in Gaza and the West Bank, Arafat would lend his *mukhabarat* (secret police) an aura of legitimacy and forge for it a constituency out of Fatah's erstwhile military cadres. The head of the PSA in Gaza is Muhammad Dahalan, former leader of the Fatah youth movement and expellee; in the West Bank, the PSA strongman is Jibril Rajoub, a Fatah activist who had served 15 years in Israeli prisons.

In December 1993, Dahalan and Rajoub met with the IDF's Deputy Chief of General Staff Amnon Shahak to sort out the modalities of their future role, both with Israeli intelligence and with the Palestinian street. Ehud Ya'ari summarised an Israeli view of the consensus that emerged from the meeting. 'Fatah-armed bands whose members were wanted by the Israeli security services, like the Hawks, will have special tasks', he wrote in January 1994. 'They will be charged with putting down any sign of opposition [to the DOP]; the intent is for them to administer show-punishments at the earliest possible stage, aimed at creating proper respect for the new regime.'[10]

Whether this was Arafat's intent was a question even Israelis could not answer. Given the limitations of Palestinian autonomy specified in the Cairo agreement, domestic opposition to it was likely to mount, requiring that Arafat have a strong internal force to curb it. But Arafat had other motives for possessing a strong PSA.

First, the PSA provided him a vital means of political patronage. His decision to disband the Hawks had left a large and potentially unruly political lobby which, if excluded from the spoils of self-government, could prove disruptive. Their absorption into the PSA paid them a wage and afforded them a political and social status to compensate for their former role as fighters. Second, no sooner had Arafat established the PSA than he broke it up into five competing blocs, each with a different 'head'. Arafat was rehearsing in the autonomy a characteristic method of his rule, tried and tested in Lebanon and Tunis, of one boss but many franchises. By allowing each agency to compete for political turf among themselves, Arafat preserved for himself the role of arbiter and prevented alternative centres of power from coalescing – a crucial task given the dissension Oslo had caused within Fatah. Finally, the shadowy, factional and lawless nature of the PSA allowed Arafat maximum leverage in his dealings with the Palestinian opposition, and particularly the Islamists.

Under the PNA

On 20 May 1994, Arafat issued a decree which annulled all laws enacted after Israel's 1967 occupation of the West Bank and Gaza, including some 2000 military orders specified by the Cairo agreement to be the 'legal framework' for the interim period. Rabin dismissed the edict as 'utterly meaningless', but in Gaza and Jericho Palestinian lawyers and judges took note, ignoring all reference to Israeli martial law. Instead, they invoked either *shari'a* for civil cases and British, Jordanian and Egyptian laws for criminal cases. This gave the PSA a free hand to deal with 'internal Palestinian security', since they were operating in a legal black hole. 'There are worrying signs that the PNA can simply round up people according to their political or religious beliefs rather than on proper legal grounds', said Palestinian human rights lawyer Raji Sourani.[11]

The dangers of such legal latitude swiftly became apparent. In the months after the PNA's installation, Palestinian lawyers in Gaza admitted that they had knowledge of 'scores' of cases, including one where a Palestinian had 'died in custody', where PNA security personnel had used torture against civilians, either for the catch-all charge of 'collaboration' or more generally for 'social' offences such as alcoholism, drug-dealing or adultery.[12] In the West Bank, PSA activists allied with Rajoub fought out a series of turf wars with rival Fatah fractions in Tulkarm, Qalqilya and Nablus, leaving at least one dead and 50 to 70 injured.[13] Fatah 'internal security units' also intervened to 'settle' land, clan and 'honour' disputes in East Jerusalem, Ramallah and Jericho. The drive behind this crackdown was twofold: to cleanse Fatah of its Oslo dissidents and to prepare the West Bank for the new 'national' dispensation. The IDF, significantly, gave both Rajoub (whose 'jurisdiction' was formally confined to Jericho) and Dahalan a free rein.

There was also political intimidation. On 28 July 1994, PNA police in Gaza blocked distribution of the *Al-Nahar* newspaper. The ostensible reason was that the paper lacked a licence, a spurious charge given that it was published in Jerusalem and so outside the PNA auspices. The real cause, in the words of a PNA official statement, was that the publication advocated a 'line that contradicts the national interests of the Palestinian people', a reference to *Al-Nahar*'s pro-Jordanian editorials. Meanwhile, the police issued orders banning 'all unauthorised political meetings' in Gaza and Jericho and threatened bus companies with fines if they allowed their vehicles to transport Palestinians to 'hostile' (oppositional) demonstrations.

The import of all these moves was to generate a sense of fear of the new regime. By and large, it worked. When *Al-Nahar* returned to the news-stands on 5 September 1994, it swore fealty to 'our brother, leader and symbol Abu Ammar [Arafat]'. The other Palestinian daily, *Al-Quds*, gave uncritical support to the PNA in general and Arafat in particular, and steadily reduced its coverage of the Palestinian opposition. Palestinian human rights organisations, particularly those tied to the PNA or based in Gaza, became more defensive, caught between a professional adherence to universal principles and the pragmatic need to protect their institutions. In the wake of *Al-Nahar*'s closure, the PSA's Moral Guidance Division issued a statement warning Palestinians not to be taken in by 'Western schools of thought ... which justify antagonistic policies toward the third world by bringing up freedom of opinion, democracy and human rights. This is a futile attempt to strike at the national authority.'

The Islamist opposition posed the PNA's security forces with their hardest task. This was reflected in semi-public rows between the 'outside' PLA and the 'inside' PSA on how best to treat Hamas. While Yusuf and Jabali favoured a strong-arm approach to crush the Islamists once and for all, Dahalan and Rajoub, mindful of Hamas's base in the territories, urged a policy aimed at splitting the movement's political and military wings. Thus on his return Arafat reputedly offered Hamas five ministries in the PNA.[14]

Hamas and the PLO

Neither approach persuaded the Islamists. While forswearing any armed conflict with the PNA, Hamas leader Mahmoud Zahar reaffirmed the movement's position as one of 'not participating in the PNA or in anything else related to the Oslo agreement'. As for attacking Israeli targets in Gaza, he added, 'this is something we announced [we would do] before and during the signing of the agreements between the PLO and Israel'. There was, in other words, an unwritten understanding that Hamas would continue its armed attacks against settlements and military installations even inside the autonomy area.

On 14 August 1994, in two separate operations outside Gaza's Gush Qatif settlement, Hamas guerrillas killed one Israeli and injured five, opening the split between the PNA's police and intelligence branches.

Yusuf ordered the arrest of 20 Hamas activists; Dahalan stepped in and had them released. 'The political leadership should identify a clear-cut policy on how to deal with the armed opposition elements and use of weapons', said a furious Yusuf. Far from steadying relations between the PNA and Hamas, these confused signals satisfied no one, with Hamas 'moderates' privately complaining that agreements with the PNA were not worth the paper they were written on and 'radicals' smelling a PLO/Israeli conspiracy to entrap them. The Israelis were livid. 'The entire agreement with the PLO is predicated on the understanding that the PLO must combat terrorism and its perpetrators', said Rabin. 'If Yassir Arafat is unable to fulfil his part, why should Israel continue implementing agreements when there is no certainty that he could later comply with them?'

On 11 October 1994, Hamas's military wing, the Izzadin al-Qassim brigades, announced that it had abducted an Israeli soldier, Nachshon Waxman, and would kill him unless 200 Palestinians prisoners were released from Israeli jails. Persuaded by security advisers that the soldier was being held in Gaza, Rabin placed the blame squarely at Arafat's door. 'You and the PNA', he told the PLO leader, 'are responsible for what happens in the territories under your control'. Arafat convened a meeting of his Higher Security Council, warning darkly that he would not abide any 'attempts aimed at embarrassing the PNA'.

Over the next five days, and despite the fact there was no evidence to suggest that Waxman was in Gaza, Palestinian police rounded up 350 Hamas 'suspects' without charge or reference to any due process of law. They 'severely interrogated' Palestinian journalists on the hunch that since they had received Hamas's message about the kidnapping they must know the provenance of the messenger. Even more ominously, there were genuine grounds to suspect that information extracted from these detainees had been passed on to Israeli intelligence.[15] Meanwhile, Gazans lived an old/new reality reminiscent of the worst days of the occupation, with roadblocks, identity checks and Hamas strongholds like the Islamic University closed on wholly political grounds.

The revelation that Waxman was not in Gaza, and never had been, merely confirmed a general Palestinian perception that Arafat had finally and unequivocally donned the role of junior partner in Rabin's furious clampdown. 'Arafat has become Lahad', scrawled graffiti in Gaza, referring to the head of the Israeli client militia in southern Lebanon. It was a street wisdom that redounded entirely to Hamas's benefit. 'Since the PNA began, it has been under Israel's wing, but this was on paper', said Zahar after the Waxman debacle.

'Now it has become a working reality. Hamas has just enjoyed a stunning success, the PNA a stunning failure.'

The failure was not lost on the Israelis. On 19 October 1994, partly to avenge the IDF's botched rescue mission in which Waxman and his three Islamist abductors were killed, a Hamas suicide bomber blew himself up in a bus in downtown Tel Aviv, killing 22 Israelis and injuring scores – the single most deadly attack in Israel for nearly 20 years. This time Rabin did not accuse the PNA. Rather, he said, Israel itself was going 'to pull the trigger ... on the terrorists'.

Rabin's policy whereby the PLO would police Palestinians on Israel's behalf was looking increasingly ragged. Both the Waxman kidnapping and the Tel Aviv bombing demonstrated that neither Arafat nor his 'strong Palestinian police' commanded the governance or the legitimacy to quell Palestinian resistance. Security would henceforth be as much Israel's business in the autonomy as Arafat's. This, in the opinion of many Israelis and Palestinians, was Oslo's inevitable dénouement. 'Where the PNA is unable to prevent attacks against Israeli settlements or Israelis so that their security is threatened, Israel may take all measures necessary to respond to such events, including the introduction of additional military forces', stated the Cairo agreement.

On 2 November 1994, an Islamic Jihad activist in Gaza, Hani Abed, opened his car door and triggered an enormous explosion. All Palestinian groups, including Fatah, were convinced his assassination bore the fingerprints of an Israeli hit job. When, the next day, Arafat tried to join Abed's funeral procession, the crowd denounced him as a traitor. A week later, in a bleakly predictable aftermath, Jihad member Hisham Hamad detonated himself outside Gaza's Netzarim settlement, killing three IDF soldiers. At a 'crisis' meeting in Madrid, Rabin reportedly told Arafat that any more incidents like Netzarim and the IDF would 'fire indiscriminately' on Palestinians in Gaza 'regardless' of the Palestinian police.[16]

The confused lines that had characterized the PNA's relations with its truculent Islamist opposition were becoming so bloody as to be meaningless. 'We have been very patient with ... the Hamas and Islamic Jihad thugs ... in the face of repeated provocations', said a PSA operative after Netzarim. 'They have escalated their attacks against Israel in order to undermine and embarrass the PNA ... From now on they should know that there is only one authority.'

On 18 November 1994, 200 Palestinian police and PSA members converged on Gaza's central Palestine Mosque to head off an Islamist demonstration. Inexplicably, they opened fire on the worshippers. The upshot was running street battles between police and civilians all over Gaza which, by the end of the day, had claimed 13 lives and left more than 200 wounded, the highest daily toll of fatalities in Gaza in 27 years of occupation. In trying to take the street the police had lost it, risking civil war in the process.

Arafat summoned a meeting of Fatah leaders in Gaza. There was only one power on the street and that was Hamas, he told them, and it was Fatah's job to do something about it.[17] On 20 November, Fatah issued a ferocious statement accusing Hamas and Jihad not only of orchestrating the 'Palestine Mosque massacre', but of assassinating eight of the 13 victims because they were 'Fatah activists'. The following day, Fatah staged a rally in Gaza City that was less a sign of 'national reconciliation' than a massive show of factional might. Motorcades of armed Fatah militants trawled through Gaza, toting machine guns and denouncing the 'hellish plot' hatched by the Islamists against 'the authority'. And Arafat poured oil on the flames: 'We will not let conspirators who receive their orders from outside destroy the Palestinians' dream of a homeland', he cried to the 10,000-strong crowd. 'The Fatah movement is the protector of security, and you and the forces of the PNA ... must work to protect this land'.

Having witnessed the collapse of his 'official' police force on 18 November, Arafat had made recourse to his last remaining constituency, Fatah and its supposedly disbanded but now re-empowered armed wing, the Fatah Hawks. He turned what had been a confrontation between the PNA and the people into a factional fight between Fatah and Hamas, and did so to save his political skin. 'It was a skilful move for a militia leader', commented Haidar Abd al-Shafi, 'but a disastrous one for a statesman'. The Israelis, though, quietly applauded this belated assertion of Arafat's authority in Gaza. 'The clashes signal that Arafat will no longer tolerate the Islamist opposition', said Yossi Sarid. 'He now understands that it's either him or them.'

For most Palestinians the 'authority' was now clearly one faction and its guns. Arafat's decision to factionalise his rule appeared to bring to fruition Rabin's terrible prophecy of a year previously. 'I prefer the Palestinians to cope with the problem of enforcing order in the Gaza Strip', Rabin had said in September 1993.

The Palestinians will be better at it than we were because they will allow no appeals to the Supreme Court and will prevent the Israeli Association of Civil Rights from criticising the conditions there by denying it access to the area. They will rule by their own methods, freeing, and this is most important, the Israeli army soldiers from having to do what they will do.[18]

There remained, however, two imponderables: would Palestinians consent to such an 'authority' and would Fatah submit to such a role?

The Struggle for Elections

Many Palestinians had backed the DOP, whatever their other misgivings, because of its pledge to hold 'direct, free and general political elections' for the PNA. Coupled with Israel's linked commitment to redeploy its military forces in Gaza and the West Bank, the prospect of a national suffrage held perhaps the greatest potential prize of the autonomy. 'This is the real challenge', said one Palestinian politically engaged academic in October 1993, 'to fight for democracy in Palestine'.[19]

Eighteen months down the road, that fight has yet to be joined, though there are signs that it is beginning. The delay is not just due to the IDF's reluctance to redeploy its forces in the West Bank, especially after Arafat's disastrous attempts at imposing 'internal security' in Gaza. It is also due to an unresolved Palestinian–Israeli dispute over the political nature of any elected Palestinian Council.

Israel wants elections for a small executive chamber with limited legislative authority. This, it figures, will bypass the 'problem' of Palestinians electing a Council not committed to the DOP, since no opposition force is likely to stand on such terms. The PLO, however, demands a 100-seat parliament with independent legislative and executive powers. Both readings are consonant with the ambiguous formulations of the DOP, but each has entirely different implications for self-rule. 'In the DOP, the PNA has both executive and legislative rights', Bashir Barghouti explains,

> If the PLO negotiators succeed in obtaining a legislative council to watch over the PNA, elections will be meaningful because Palestinians will be able to practise power freely. But if the elections are for an executive council only, they will be a formality because any legislation passed ... would have to go to a joint PLO–Israeli committee for approval.[20]

The debate over elections goes to the heart of the competing Israeli and Palestinian versions of autonomy, and sets up what will probably be the most significant political struggle of the interim period. Either Israel will succeed in imposing on the Palestinians an autonomy whose primary goal is to secure Israel's security and territorial interests, or the Palestinians will manage to wrest the rudiments of a law-based democratic polity to resist the Israeli vision and lay the bases for future national sovereignty.

The realisation of an elected and independent legislature would give the PNA a popular legitimacy it currently lacks, and could create a focus for a coalition united around the goals of independence, democracy and development. While Hamas leaders have repeatedly signalled that they will have no truck with any 'Arafat appointed executive', they have been ambivalent about participating in an independent legislature. The lure is obvious: legislative influence over the civic spheres of education, social welfare and the family would be difficult for the Islamists to turn down, even if the price was renunciation of armed struggle.[21] Many Palestinian independent and even oppositional forces have predicated their own participation in the PNA on the extent of the legislative and democratic sway it enjoys. 'Not until elections become a reality, and all posts within the administration are seen to be accountable', said Raji Sourani, 'will the populace be completely confident with the PNA'.[22]

Is this Arafat's scenario? From the moment the PLO leader returned to Palestine, he has insistently called for elections. Many believe his preferred option would be a presidential vote, garnering for him and his administration a popular mandate while leaving his autocratic powers intact. These suspicions are grounded not just on the ambiguities of the DOP or the vagaries of the PLO's own Basic Law, but even more so on Arafat's practice since he took up his 'presidency'.

Virtually Arafat's first act on installation of the PNA was to appoint its 20 ministers. The 'cabinet' amounts to a political bloc between loyal elements of his Tunis bureaucracy, such as Nabil Sha'th and Intissar al-Wazir, and representatives of Palestine's traditional elite families, such as Muhammad Nashashibi and Munib Masri, none of whom has any popular base in the territories. With the exception of two ministers drawn from the small but pro-Oslo Fida party, the cabinet's political complexion is either Fatah or, as one observer put it, 'independently Fatah'.

If Arafat could claim expediency for his appointees given the 'temporary' nature of the cabinet – in place, according to the DOP, only until PNA elections are held – no such pretext could explain his dealings with Palestinian municipalities in the territories. In the run-up to the PNA's establishment, Gaza mayor Mansur Shawwa had appointed a provisional municipal council that enjoyed the support of all PLO factions, the Islamist movements, and representatives of Gaza's refugee, landowner and professional sectors. The consensus had been achieved on the bases of two conditions. First, the municipality would concern itself solely with the delivery of public services rather than 'political contests' over Oslo. Second, the council would take immediate steps to prepare for proper municipal elections. 'If these conditions are not met', said Shawwa, 'I won't agree to head the council, because it won't be able to fulfil its responsibilities. I hope the president understands this.'

Arafat, on his return to Gaza, not only rejected Shawwa's list but replaced him and his appointed councillors with nine persons known only for their fidelity to the PLO leader. In Nablus, Arafat ousted opposition councillors by polarising the municipality over the question of support for Oslo. These moves alarmed many Palestinians not simply because of the caprice of Arafat's appointments, but because of the precedent they set for any future general elections. 'Arafat is appointing city councils for one-year terms', said former peace talks delegate Ghassan Khatib. 'That proves that local elections will not be held for at least a year, and general elections will come even later.'[23]

These fears were compounded by Arafat's apparent disinterest in the fate of his own Fatah movement in the territories. He had allowed the virtual political disintegration of Fatah in the period after Oslo; and his blueprint for its future role seemed to be that of a Ba'th-like ruling party whose personnel would be indistinguishable from the functionaries that staffed the PNA's civil and military structures.[24] The transformation of the Fatah Hawks into preventive security operatives, and Rajoub and Dahalan's crackdown on Fatah's more independently minded cadres, appeared to bear out these prognoses. It was a trend that was bound to resist the generation of Fatah activists politically schooled in the territories, given that their reservations about Oslo made them wary of any straight equation of 'movement' with 'authority'. 'We must draw clear lines of demarcation between Fatah and the PNA', said West Bank Fatah leader Marwan Barghouti.[25]

In November 1994, in Ramallah, Fatah organised elections for its local leadership, the first in a series of 'primaries' to be held throughout the West Bank and ultimately in Gaza and Jericho. Arafat reportedly neither endorsed nor criticised the process, but he could hardly have been happy with the political divisions within Fatah thrown up by the campaign, nor with its results. While one list allied with Jibril Rajoub stood on a ticket of 'national unity' with the PNA, a second list aligned itself with the outside Fatah 'dissident' leader Hani al-Hasan, supporting the DOP but opposing the Cairo agreement. More significantly, the 'dissidents' fought to keep Fatah as a national movement independent of the PNA, one that would, if the peace process collapsed, resume its struggle against the occupation.[26]

In the poll of 583 members, the Fatah dissidents scored a resounding victory: not a single member of Rajoub's (that is Arafat's) list gained a place on the 15-seat executive. The results also showed up major sectoral divisions in the movement, with the majority of positions going to ex-prisoners, refugees and villagers as opposed to Arafat's preferred 'notable' and 'resident' appointees.

One week after the Ramallah verdict, Arafat announced that no further 'internal' elections would be held until the PNA was in place in the West Bank and the Israeli army redeployed. The PLO leader had read the writing on the wall. Not only did the Ramallah results reveal just how low his stock had sunk in the eyes of his own followers; they also marked the opening shot in what is likely to be a political battle for Fatah's soul, one that could put his own leadership on the line and irrevocably fracture the movement's hitherto hegemonic position into contending political and class blocs. Many observers believe the very fact of elections signalled an attempt by the younger Fatah leadership inside the territories to wrest control from the Tunis leadership whom they blame, far more than they blame Arafat personally, for the PNA's dismal performance in Gaza and Jericho. It also shows, said Marwan Barghouti, that many in Fatah have registered the changed meaning of legitimacy that the combined experiences of Israeli occupation, the intifada and self-rule has wrought in modern Palestinian political consciousness. 'In the past Fatah earned its right to lead the national movement by virtue of the military struggle of its fighters and the blood of its martyrs', he said. 'Now we have a PNA on Palestinian soil [and] we must earn our legitimacy from the democratic choice of the people'.

These sentiments place the Fatah dissidents in the same political camp as the Palestine People's Party, Fida and those independents associated with Haidar Abd al-Shafi's reform movement. Were they to combine their forces into some kind of united front, they would comprise what Jamal Hilal has called a 'democratic-secular bloc', a potential third force in Palestinian politics able to steer a course between the autocratic drift of Arafat's coalition of ex-Tunis bureaucrats and Palestine's landowning elites on the one hand and the sectarian rejectionism advocated by Hamas on the other. Should they also fight to revitalise the PLO's national programme via the democratic reform of its institutions, such a bloc is likely to draw to itself elements from the influential but currently marginalised Popular and

Democratic Fronts, as well as support from Palestine's women's and labour movements and NGOs.

Do these constituencies possess either the organisational capacity or political will to mount a challenge to Arafat? The 'reform movement' around Abd al-Shafi has so far confined itself to circulating a series of important but politically ineffectual petitions. In May 1994, 25 personalities representing the territories' independent and NGO sectors issued a statement denouncing the Cairo agreement and calling on Palestinians 'not to comply' with it. In August, 171 'prominent Palestinians', including 82 members of the PNC, swore to resist any change to the Palestinian National Charter, declaring that Arafat no longer had 'the authority to speak in the name of the PLO or commit it to anything'. Signatories included not only independents like Haidar Abd al-Shafi and Edward Said but also Fatah's Farouq Qaddumi and Hani al-Hasan and the PFLP and DFLP leaders George Habash and Nayif Hawatmeh.

These battles for the soul of Palestinian nationalism have an ideological resonance among Palestinians, but they are unlikely to check Arafat's rule in the autonomy unless backed up by organised opposition on the ground. The forum for this fight, said Ghassan Khatib, must be over the content and form of the PNA elections. 'There are enough indications that neither the Palestinian [leadership] nor the Israeli side is serious about elections', he said. 'And since the democracy and participation that could come out of elections will not be given, the social and political forces must work to take them.'[27]

Khatib believes that a popular struggle for elections would provide the 'vital key' through which Palestinian civil and political society could renew itself and escape the crisis that has cumulatively beset it since Oslo. First, elections would strengthen the PLO's negotiating position vis-à-vis the Israelis by anchoring it in a mass-mobilised base. Second, elections would create a political catalyst that would unite Palestine's currently disparate political, social and regional forces, and would also set off a 'democratic dynamic' throughout Palestinian society, emboldening it to construct genuinely national institutions beyond the reach of the constrictions imposed by the DOP, Israel or its own leadership. Finally, given the *de facto* obsolescence of the PLO, elections would restore legitimacy to the fight for Palestinian self-determination, instigating some form of accountability between 'the nation and its leaders'.

It is this national dimension that, in the opinion of Palestinian intellectual Azmi Bishara, makes a mass struggle for elections the central strategic objective for Palestinians in the interim period. Bishara outlines a two-pronged approach. The first aims to use the

Palestinians struggle for democracy against and within the PNA. The second aims to

> re-politicis[e] the Palestinian case which has been disfigured and converted into an administrative case in Oslo and Cairo, and restor[e] its national dimension by putting forward expressions of sovereignty and people's will, dimensions that are missing from Oslo/Cairo ... Elections open up again the issue of sovereignty as linked to democracy.[28]

7

Epilogue: Bitter Fruits, Bitter Truths

In 1984, in a seminal essay on Israel and the Palestinians, Eqbal Ahmad reflected on the legitimacy the PLO has historically commanded, not just among the Palestinians but also 'among perhaps the largest mass of people in the Third World'.[1] He suggested that the reason was not only the identification with the justice and simplicity of the Palestinians' cause – that of an exiled people's quest for a homeland. It was, rather, that of all the national liberation struggles, the PLO had been the 'most successful' in steering worldwide attention to its case. Ahmad called the PLO 'the only political movement in recorded history which is formally recognised by more governments throughout the world than its governmental adversary'. It was a legitimacy enshrined in numerous UN resolutions and overwhelmingly endorsed at various international fora, including the 1989 UN General Assembly where Resolution 242 'along with the right of self-determination of the Palestinians' was passed 151 votes to three.[2] On this issue at least, wrote John Pilger, 'there is no greater international consensus'.[3] The paradox, of course, was that the PLO had been 'strikingly unsuccessful' in wresting back from Israel a single inch of the land taken from its people first in 1948, and then again in 1967.

After Oslo, that paradox no longer holds. The PLO has a national authority in Gaza and Jericho, with autonomy over 6.6 per cent of mandate Palestine and the promise of extending this limited form of self-government over 'Palestinian population centres' in the West Bank. But it has achieved this by abandoning the international consensus to throw in its lot with those whom Noam Chomsky has termed 'the real rejectionists' on the question of Palestine – Israel and the US.[4]

Wherever the Oslo-inspired peace process eventually leads, it is clear that its conditions are now these. In pursuit of Israeli and US recognition of its representative status, the PLO – or rather Arafat and the tiny cabal of loyalists around him – agreed to shelve the movement's national goals of Israeli withdrawal and Palestinian self-determination and return, which had invested it with representative legitimacy. 'The Palestinians have done their historic duty of saying yes' to the new US/Israeli order for the Middle East, said Rashid Khalidi in November 1993.[5] What has been gained?

In the period since Oslo, PLO representatives, intentionally or otherwise, have largely given away the essence of the Palestinian position 'on the basis of which Palestinian national rights had gained worldwide recognition during the past quarter of a century'.[6] On three of the crucial components of that position – settlements, refugees, and international protection of Palestinians in the occupied territories – it is now the Israeli rather than the Palestinian interpretation that prevails, both in the territories where it always had the power of military force and internationally, where it did not.

By agreeing to defer the question of settlements and Jerusalem until the permanent status talks, and by trusting to Rabin's purely verbal pledge to maintain Israel's 'freeze' on new settlement starts in the territories, the PLO leadership has helped to conceal, domestically and internationally, an actual Israeli expansion of settlements in the West Bank that is now proceeding, according to Israeli commentators, at three times the pace of settlement construction under the Shamir government.[7] Since Oslo, Israel has confiscated a further 40,000 acres of Palestinian land, targeting in particular 'Greater Jerusalem' and the existing settlements along the old Green Line, in effect preemptively redrawing Israel's pre-1967 borders eastwards. It has also embarked on the building of a 400km network of 'settler roads' in the West Bank and Gaza that will, for security purposes, be off-limits to Palestinians. The eventual territorial dispensation this augurs for any future Palestinian entity has been chillingly sketched by Meron Benvenisti. 'These decisions', he said, 'have already disconnected the West Bank into two separate cantons ... and will turn a huge expanse – about 10 percent of the entire West Bank – into a region in which it will be impossible to implement any final arrangement except by annexation to Israel'.[8]

The fate of the 1.8 million Palestinian refugees who reside outside the territories has also taken a sharp turn for the worse since Oslo. In confining negotiations to those Palestinians 'displaced' in 1967, PLO negotiators have become mired in debates with Israel over the numbers and modalities of their return but have forsaken the principle that all refugees, by virtue of being refugees, are legally entitled to return or be compensated. The refugee question has thus ceased to be a matter of international law and is, rather, subject to negotiations between Israel, the PNA and the refugees' host countries. This is a long-sought Israeli objective, massively bolstered by the 1993 and 1994 votes in the UN General Assembly against all resolutions pertaining to Palestinian refugees because 'such resolutions prejudge the outcome of the ongoing peace process and should be solved by direct negotiations'.[9] Direct negotiations, given the pressure Israel and the US can bring to bear, are likely to remove the basis of the refugees' case, especially those expelled in 1948. At best they will gain offers of permanent settlement in their host countries; at worst, further dispersal.[10]

The most crucial shortcoming is that since Oslo Israel has succeeded in imposing, and getting, PLO and international covenant for a definition of 'peace' that rests on unconditional security for Israel but extremely conditional security for the Palestinians, both under occupation and in the diaspora. By the spring of 1995, all movement on issues relating to the interim period – Israel's military redeployment in the West Bank, PNA elections, or even the relaxation of collective punishments (like closure of the territories) – hinged, in Shimon Peres's words, on 'Arafat taking care of terror'. The upshot has been a repressive Israeli regime of containment that since Oslo has killed 255 Palestinians in the West Bank and Gaza, while attacks by Palestinians have claimed 137 Israelis. Israel has resorted to mass punitive measures such as the arrest of 2400 Palestinians for alleged 'Islamist sympathies' between October 1994 and January 1995. Over the same period, in the autonomous enclaves of Gaza and Jericho, PNA security forces have undertaken five mass arrest campaigns, rounding up hundreds of Palestinians affiliated with PLO and Islamist opposition groups without 'judicial warrant or sanction and ... contrary to the rule of law'.[11] In February 1995, the PNA established special military courts to try such political suspects, a move which, in the opinion of human rights lawyer, Raji Sourani, undermines 'the independence of the judiciary' and marks the 'beginning of a trend towards the militarisation of Palestinian society'.[12] Sourani was pulled in for 16 hours of 'questioning' after making that statement.

It would be easy to lay the blame for this state of affairs at the door of Yasir Arafat. Yet no matter how autocratic, corrupt and authoritarian the PLO is, and no matter how integral Arafat remains to Palestinian nationalism, the cause of the political defeat that Oslo now signifies cannot be so easily fixed. It is the bitter fruit of the structure of politics for which the PLO leadership and virtually all factions, including the opposition factions, bear a historic responsibility.[13]

The PLO has tended to view diplomacy strategically rather than tactically. As a result, the PLO has repeatedly conferred on the US the role of just and even-handed arbiter, rather than recognise it as an imperial power with its own interests and ambitions. In that process, the PLO largely conceded what Ghassan Khatib has termed the 'strategic factors in its favour' that could have, had they been properly deployed, partially compensated for the negotiations' built-in imbalance of power.[14] One such factor is an insistence that the reference points for any negotiations remain those UN Resolutions, specifically 242 and 338, which stipulate the principles of land for peace and the illegality of occupation. Furthermore, and on these bases, the PLO should have maintained the principle of Arab coordination. However risky this was during the Madrid phase, it at least sustained the status quo ante of no normalisation of relations with Israel except in the framework of a comprehensive solution. With Oslo – and because of Arafat's solo diplomacy – this was broken, a breach that has redounded entirely to Israel's benefit. As a result, Syria and Lebanon have been isolated, the Arabs' secondary and tertiary economic boycott of Israel has been lifted, and Israel has realised its second peace treaty with a frontline Arab state (Jordan in August 1994). If Arafat expected a degree of political rehabilitation for this gesture, he has been sorely disappointed. The PLO is now dependent diplomatically on Egypt, estranged from Syria and Lebanon, and in virtual competition with Jordan for Israeli political and economic favours.

Secondly, Arafat and the PLO leadership viewed the move to Gaza and Jericho as a staging post to get the West Bank, rather than an opportunity to found a law-based, democratic Palestinian political entity in readiness for the interim period. Thus, the PLO is left lacking all of those preconditions needed for it to get the international, Arab and Palestinian support that would enable the PNA to build a genuinely popular constituency for the process: a legal and regulatory investment framework, an open and participatory development programme, and a functioning, transparent fiscal system.[15] In its stead, there is a patrimonial system of government in which 'corruption, kickbacks, mismanagement and, ultimately, economic and political failure' are the norm.[16] The upshot is that the only leverage Arafat now has vis-à-vis Israel is an ever more ruthless implementation of the latter's 'internal security' agenda, with all the negative consequences this has for Palestinian democracy and human rights.

Finally, there is the sheer lack of accountability of a movement which, at last count, placed no less than 60 semi-governmental functions under the sole prerogative of one man. Arafat decides on everything, from the modalities of donors' aid programmes to who in Gaza receives a telephone line. Such concentration of power may have been necessary to keep the PLO afloat during its long years of exile, but, as Naseer Aruri laments, it is 'simply at variance with the requirements of efficiency and rational decision-making' in a period of nascent state formation.[17]

How the Palestinians will pursue their historic claim of self-determination on the irreversibly altered terrain of Oslo is now an open proposition. But one thing is clear. Those claims cannot be realised either with the PLO as it is presently constituted or with Arafat solely at the helm. This may appear unthinkable when one considers the symbiosis that has historically characterised the relationship between the PLO, Arafat and Palestinian nationalism. 'Having lost the goal of national liberation', Azmi Bishara observed in October 1994, 'the legitimacy of the present Palestinian leadership does not derive from this goal, that is the future, but from history that is the past'.[18]

When and how the struggle for a new Palestinian leadership will unfold cannot now be predicted. Any new leadership that emerges will have to address two cardinal issues. First, it will have to reformulate Palestinian nationalism according to the changed realities of the post-Oslo and post-Cold War world, and then base that nationalism on the vision of a non-sectarian, democratic and independent future. The path to self-determination cannot, in the end, be a 'junior partnership' with Israel. Coexistence based on such disproportionate political and economic relations of power and subordination denies the possibility of an authentic national sovereignty, no matter what trappings of statehood a future Palestinian entity may enjoy. Second, Palestinians must continue and reinvigorate their arduous struggle to build a law-based and democratic political culture in which to express their nationalism. This means elections not just for the PNA, but also for the municipalities, professional associations, unions, women's committees, PLO factions and the array of institutions that comprise Palestinian civil society in the territories and in the diaspora. And it means developing a democratic practice.[19]

'I tell you plainly that the negotiations are not worth fighting about', said Haidar Abd al-Shafi in 1993.

> The critical issue is transforming our society. All else is inconsequential ... We must decide amongst ourselves to use our strength and resources to develop our collective leadership and the democratic institutions which will achieve our goals and guide us in the future ... The important thing is for us to take care of our internal situation and correct those negative aspects from which it has been suffering for generations and which is the main reason for our losses against our foes.[20]

If the dual goals of national unity and national liberation are to be achieved, the Palestinian struggle, as Abd al-Shafi implies, will have to be strategically consistent but tactically virtuoso. That struggle needs to be waged both through Oslo and against it, both within the current PLO leadership and, inevitably, in opposition to it. The reason is obvious. Palestinian self-determination does not lie in the terms of the Oslo-sponsored peace process. It lies, rather, in the still to be contested social, democratic, economic, institutional, and international spaces that Oslo may, if politically and responsibly exploited, open up.

References

Foreword

1. For more on this, see Usher's chapter in Joel Beinin and Joe Stork, eds, *Political Islam: Essays from Middle East Report* (Berkeley and Los Angeles: University of California Press, Spring 1996).
2. Readers who wish to follow Palestine–Israel developments should consult the ongoing coverage in *Middle East Report* and Usher's first-rate reporting in *Middle East International* (MEI). MEI also features excellent coverage of PLO affairs by Lamis Andoni and of Israeli affairs by Haim Baram and other Israeli writers. From the 'inside' we would recommend the weekly *Palestine Report* of the Jerusalem Media and Communications Centre (JMCC) and the publications of the Alternative Information Centre, also based in Jerusalem, which publishes *News From Within* (monthly) and *The Other Front* (weekly).
3. On the historic 'rejection' of US policy see Noam Chomsky, *The Fateful Triangle: the United States, Israel and the Palestinians* (Boston: South End Press, 1983). See also Joe Stork, 'US Policy and the Palestine Question', in Hooshang Amirahmadi, ed., *The United States and the Middle East* (Albany: State University of New York Press, 1993) and 'The Clinton Administration and the Palestine Question' in Michael W. Suleiman, ed., *US Policy on Palestine from Wilson to Clinton* (Normal, Il: Association of Arab-American University Graduates, 1995).
4. Jewish settlers account for less than 15 per cent of the West Bank's population, and less than one per cent of Gaza's. In 1994, the settler population grew by approximately 10.5 per cent, a slight increase from the year before but less than the 12 per cent in 1992, and 15 per cent in 1991 (*Report on Israeli Settlements in the Occupied Territories*, January 1995). The Palestinian National Authority estimates that Israel has confiscated more than 20 square miles between September 1993 and January 1995 (*New York Times*, 16 January 1995). The JMCC gives a 13-month estimate of 57 square miles, including 'closed military areas' and 'nature reserves' (*Palestine Report*, 31 December 1994). This is 2.3 per cent of the Occupied Territories, and higher than the 2.1 per cent average annual rates of confiscation since 1967.

The number of Jewish settlers in the West Bank is now about 160,000 (not including Jerusalem), and about 5000 in Gaza. According to Israel Shahak, one of Israel's foremost critics of the occupation, some 70 per cent of the West Bank is state land, of which 16 per cent has been allocated to Jewish settlements. Not only have no settlements been vacated, there has been not even a partial restitution of the remaining 54 per cent as a means of boosting Palestinian public support for the 'self-rule' scheme. See *Shahak Report* 154 (12 May 1995).

5. *Financial Times*, 12 May 1995).
6. Tel Aviv University professor Tania Reinhart has argued that the Gaza–Jericho arrangement compares not with the end of apartheid rule in South Africa but rather with the 1959 Law for the Advancement of the Independent Government of the Bantu People (*Ha-Aretz* weekend supplement, 27 May 1994; translation in *The Other Front*, 31 May 1994). An Israeli Peace Bloc (Gush Shalom) advertisement in *Ha-Aretz* (2 February 1995) noted that the Hebrew term for 'separation' – Rabin's term for the solution to the problem of violent Palestinian attacks on Israeli troops and individuals – 'is the exact Hebrew translation for the South African term apartheid' (Cited in Graham Usher, 'Palestinian trade unions and the struggle for independence', *Middle East Report* 194/195 [May–August 1995], p. 24).
7. See Graham Usher's interview with Marwan Barghouti in *Middle East Report* 189 (July–August 1994). It must be said, however, that Barghouti was a full accomplice in Arafat's successful campaign to undermine a month-long Palestinian prisoner's strike in June–July 1995. This was one of the most striking instances of the Palestinian National Authority's concern to demobilize and divide resurgences of Palestinian grassroots struggle.
8. Bishara's remarks at Tel Aviv University symposium are in *News From Within*, July 1995, pp. 14–16.

Chapter 1

1. The four documents are: the three PLO–Israeli letters of mutual recognition, Tunis and Jerusalem, 9 September 1993 (Arafat to Rabin, Arafat to Norwegian Foreign Minister Johan Jurgen Holst and Rabin to Arafat). The fourth text is the Israeli–PLO Declaration of Principles, Washington, DC, 13 September 1993. These are reproduced in the *Journal of Palestine Studies* 23, 1 (Autumn 1993) pp. 114–24.
2. Andrew Gowers and Tony Walker, *Arafat: the Biography*, second edition (London: Virgin, 1994) p. 472.
3. Bernard Sabella, 'Russian Jewish immigration and the future of the Israeli–Palestinian conflict', *Middle East Report*, May–June 1993.
4. Noam Chomsky, *Deterring Democracy* (New York: Vintage, 1992).

5. Camille Mansour, 'The Palestinian–Israeli negotiations: an overview and assessment', *Journal of Palestine Studies*, Spring 1993.
6. Graham Usher, 'Life in the occupied territories after Madrid', *Middle East International*, 6 March 1992.
7. Mansour, 'The Palestinian–Israeli negotiations'.
8. Lamis Andoni, 'The PLO in the occupied territories', *Middle East International*, 4 February 1994.
9. Gowers and Walker, *Arafat*, p. 476.
10. Jamil Hilal, 'PLO Institutions: the challenge ahead', *Journal of Palestine Studies*, Autumn 1993.
11. Graham Usher, 'Israel's undercover army', *New Statesman/Society*, 4 September 1992.
12. See, for instance, the UNL's 'Fourteen Points' in Z. Schiff and E. Ya'ari, *Intifada: the Palestinian Uprising – Israel's Third Front* (New York: Simon and Schuster, 1990) p. 206.
13. Graham Usher, 'The rise of political Islam in the occupied territories', *Middle East International*, 25 June 1993.
14. The Democracy and Workers' Rights Centre, Ramallah, West Bank, 1994.
15. Quoted in 'The occupiers vs. the intifada', *Democratic Palestine*, January–March 1993.
16. Graham Usher, 'Why Gaza says yes, mostly', *Race & Class*, January–March 1993.
17. 'Mabat' [Israel TV], 30 March 1993, quoted in Tikva Honig-Parnass, 'A new stage: military intifada, Israeli panic, ruthles oppression', *News From Within*, 2 April 1993, p. 4.
18. Avi Shlaim, 'The Oslo accord', *Journal of Palestine Studies*, Spring 1994.
19. Quoted in Avi Shlaim, 'Prelude to the Accord: Likud, Labour and the Palestinians', *Journal of Palestine Studies*, Winter 1994, p. 14.
20. Hanan Ashrawi, 'The accord incorporated key concessions we couldn't get [in Washington]', *Middle East Report*, January–February 1994.
21. I owe these insights to Salim Tamari.
22. Marwan Barghouti, 'Arafat and the opposition', *Middle East Report*, November–December 1994.
23. Haidar Abd al-Shafi, 'The Oslo agreement', *Journal of Palestine Studies*, Autumn 1993.
24. See 'Delegation revived', *Palestine Report*, 8–14 August 1993.
25. Shlaim, 'The Oslo accord', p. 32.
26. Lamis Andoni, 'Packing bags for a historic, bittersweet journey', *Christian Science Monitor*, 8 June 1994.
27. Salim Tamari, 'The critics are afraid of the challenge of opposing their own bourgeoisie', *Middle East Report*, January–February 1994.
28. Abd al-Shafi, 'The Oslo agreement'.

Chapter 2

1. Mouin Rabbani, 'Arafat's fateful gamble', *Middle East International*, 10 September 1993.
2. Lamis Andoni, 'Arafat asserts his control', *Middle East International*, 22 October 1993.
3. Samir Hleileh, 'The economic protocols are the price we had to pay', *Middle East Report*, January–February 1994.
4. Graham Usher, 'Breakdown of confidence in the territories', *Middle East International*, 8 October 1993.
5. Sarah Roy, 'Gaza: new dynamics of civic disintegration', *Journal of Palestine Studies*, Summer 1993.
6. Yizhar Be'er and Saleh Abdel Jawad, *Collaborators in the Occupied Territories: Human Rights Abuses and Violations* (Jerusalem: B'Tselem, 1994) p. 168.
7. Meron Benvenisti, 'Border conflict', *Ha'aretz*, 16 December 1993.
8. *Al Quds*, 16 February 1994.
9. Quoted in *The Other Front*, 23 February 1994.
10. Ehud Ya'ari, 'No hope in shame', *Jerusalem Report*, 10 March 1994.
11. Peace Now Settlement Watch Committee, *Settlement Facts*, 1993.
12. Barghouti, 'Arafat and the opposition'.
13. Graham Usher, 'Israel's rampaging settlers', *Middle East International*, 19 November 1993.
14. The phrase is Frieh Abu Midain's, the PNA's current Justice Minister.
15. Graham Usher, 'The aftermath of Hebron', *Middle East International*, 4 March 1994.
16. Lamis Andoni, 'Arafat ignores his constituency', *Middle East International*, 1 April 1994. For text of the Cairo security agreement, see 'Israel–PLO agreements', *Journal of Palestine Studies*, Summer 1994.
17. Quoted in Graham Usher, 'Reorganising the occupation', *Middle East International*, 15 April 1994.
18. I owe this insight to Marwan Ali Kafarna.
19. For text of the 4 May 1994 Cairo agreement, see 'Israel–PLO agreements', *Journal of Palestine Studies*, Summer 1994; reproduced in this volume as Appendix 2.
20. Meron Benvenisti, 'An agreement of surrender', *Ha'aretz*, 12 May 1994.

Chapter 3

1. Ehud Ya'ari, 'Can Arafat govern?' *Jerusalem Report*, 13 January 1994.
2. Gowers and Walker, *Arafat*, p. 129.
3. Israel Shahak, 'Hamas and Arafat: the balance of power', *Middle East International*, 4 February 1994.

4. Bassam Jarrar, 'The Islamist Movement and the Palestinian Authority', *Middle East Report*, July–August 1994.

5. Danny Rubinstein, *Ha'aretz*, 21 December 1993.

6. Graham Usher, 'The PLO opposition: rebels without a constituency', *Middle East International*, 7 October 1994.

7. Thus Hamas's share of the vote in the Birzeit elections was the same as the previous year. It achieved victory through its alliance with the PFLP and DFLP.

8. Graham Usher, 'Hamas' shifting fortunes', *Middle East International*, 24 September 1993.

9. See the interview with Yasin in Be'er and Abdel Jawad, *Collaborators*, pp. 219–28.

10. Jarrar, 'The Islamist movement'.

11. Graham Usher, 'Dissension in the opposition', *Middle East International*, 22 October 1993.

12. Jarrar, 'The Islamist movement'.

13. Ibid.

14. I owe this conceptualisation of Hamas as an 'invented tradition' to Rema Hammami. See her 'Women, the Hijab and the Intifada', *Middle East Report*, May–August 1990. For a more general treatment of the concept see Eric Hobsbawm and Terence Ranger, eds, *The Invention of Tradition* (Cambridge: Cambridge University Press, 1983).

15. Khalid Suleiman Amayreh, 'Hamas debates its next move', *Middle East International*, 27 May 1994.

16. Yossi Torfstein, 'Despite the sword', *Ha'aretz*, 26 April 1994.

17. Jarrar, 'The Islamist movement'.

18. Lamis Andoni, 'Palestinian Islamist group signals shift in strategy', *Christian Science Monitor*, 13 September 1994.

19. For an account of the PNA's attempted crackdown on Hamas see Chapter 6.

20. Jamil Hilal, 'PLO institutions'.

Chapter 4

1. I owe this insight to Mark Taylor. For text of the Paris agreement, see 'Israel–PLO agreements', *Journal of Palestine Studies*, Summer 1994; reproduced in this volume as Appendix 3.

2. Statement of the first meeting of the PNA in Tunis on 30 May 1994.

3. This definition of economic sovereignty is from Stanley Fischer, 'Economic transition in the occupied territories', *Journal of Palestine Studies*, Summer 1994.

4. George Abed, 'Developing the Palestinian economy', *Journal of Palestine Studies*, Summer 1994.

5. I owe this analysis to Alex Pollock.

6. Abed, 'Developing the Palestinian economy'.
7. Salah Abd al-Shafi, 'We will be working for Israel in Gaza rather than in Tel Aviv', *Middle East Report*, January–February 1994.
8. Adel Samara, 'Israel swallowing the economy of the Palestinian cantons', *News From Within*, 5 October 1993.
9. Hisham Shawa,'Letter to the Arab League', *Al Quds*, 6 January 1994.
10. Hisham Awartani, 'Palestinian–Jordanian Agricultural Relations: contraints and prospects', *Palestine–Israel Journal*, Summer 1994.
11. For a theoretical analysis of the role of 'industrial parks' in the 'new imperialism', see A. Sivanandan, *New Circuits of Imperialism in Communities of Resistance: Writings on Black Struggles for Socialism* (London: Verso, 1990).
12. Abd al-Shafi, 'We will be working for Israel'.
13. Ibid.
14. Asher Davidi, 'Israel's strategy for Palestinian independence', *Middle East Report*, September–October 1993.
15. Ibid.
16. Abd al-Shafi, 'We will be working for Israel'.
17. Stephen Castles and Godula Kosack, *Immigrant Workers and Class Structure in Western Europe* (London, 1973).

Chapter 5

1. Nasser Aruri and John Carroll, 'A new Palestinian charter', *Journal of Palestine Studies*, Summer 1994.
2. Nasser Aruri and John Carroll, 'The draft Palestinian constitution', *Middle East International*, 15 April 1994.
3. Mustafa Barghouti, 'Aid to Arafat hurts ordinary Palestinians', *Wall Street Journal*, 30 August 1994.
4. Quoted in Eyad al-Sarraj, 'PNGOs: Challenges and changes in the coming era', *PNGO Newsletter*, October 1994.
5. Barghouti, 'Aid to Arafat'.
6. Mustafa Barghouti, *Palestinian NGOs and their Role in Building a Civil Society* (Jerusalem: Union of Palestinian Medical Relief Committees, June 1994).
7. Interview with Jamal Zaqout, October 1994.
8. Interview with Umayya Khammash, October 1994.
9. Barghouti, 'Palestinian NGOs'.
10. Barghouti, 'Palestinian NGOs'.
11. George Giacaman, 'Human rights in the throes of politics', conference paper for the First International Conference on Human Rights (Jerusalem: Land and Water Establishment for Studies and Legal Services, November 1994) p. 63.
12. Jarrar, 'The Islamist movement'.
13. Ghazi Abu Jiab, 'Arafat and the opposition', *Middle East Report*, November–December 1994.

14. Maha Nassar and Aida Issawi, in Maya Rosenfeld, 'Women of the opposition unite', *Challenge*, November–December 1993, pp. 8–10.
15. Graham Usher, 'The foul-up over Israel's Palestinian prisoners', *Middle East International*, 24 June 1994.
16. Walid Salem, 'The Palestinian democratic project – hopes and dangers', *News From Within*, May 1994.
17. Ghazi Abu Jiab, 'Reflections on the present state of the intifada: achievements and failures', *News From Within*, July 1992.
18. Hilal, 'PLO institutions'.
19. George Giacaman, 'The role of the opposition in the coming stage', *Al Quds*, 14 January 1994.
20. On the impact of the intifada on Palestinian women, see Rita Giacaman and Penny Johnson, 'Building barricades and breaking barriers', in Zachery Lockman and Joel Beinin, eds, *Intifada: the Palestinian Uprising against Israeli Occupation* (London: MERIP/I.B. Taurus, 1989).
21. Islah Jad, 'From Salons to Popular Committees', in Jamal Nassar and Roger Heacock, eds, *Intifada: Palestine at the Crossroads* (Birzeit University and New York: Praeger, 1991) pp. 138–9.
22. Interview with Islah Jad, July 1994.
23. Suha Barghouti, 'Autonomy does not respect women's rights', *Challenge*, July–August 1994.
24. I owe this information to Bassam Jarrar.
25. Interview with Jad.
25. Ibid.
26. Hanan Riyan Bakri, 'Women in Islam', *Palestine–Israel Journal*, Spring 1994.
27. Rita Giacaman, 'Palestinian women, the intifada and the state of independence', *Race & Class*, January–March 1993.
28. Suha Barghouti, 'Autonomy'.
30. Quoted in Rita Giacaman and Penny Johnson, 'Searching for strategies: the Palestinian women's movement in the new era', *Middle East Report*, January–February 1994.
31. Giacaman, 'Palestinian women'.
32. Quoted in Giacaman and Johnson, 'Searching for strategies'.
33. Interview with Jad.
34. Joost Hiltermann, 'Work and action: the role of the working class in the uprising', in Nassar and Heacock, *Intifada*, p. 145.
35. Information from the International Labour Organisation, November 1994.
36. Information from the Democracy and Workers' Rights Centre.
37. Mustafa Barghouti, 'Palestinian NGOs'.
38. I owe this information to Adnan Abu Shami and Amna Rimayeh.
39. This is the estimation of Hassan Barghouti.
40. Interview with Hassan Barghouti, October 1994.
41. Ibid.
42. Ibid.

Chapter 6

1. Nasser Aruri, 'Political paralysis in Palestine', *Middle East International*, 21 October 1994.
2. See, for instance, Samir Abdallah, 'A Marshall Plan for the Region', *News From Within*, 5 October 1993.
3. Abdallah Bouhabib, 'The World Bank and international aid to Palestine', *Journal of Palestine Studies*, Winter 1994.
4. Ibid.
5. 'Businessmen demand reform', *Palestine Report*, 21 December 1993.
6. Graham Usher, 'The riot at the Erez checkpoint', *Middle East International*, 22 July 1994.
7. Quoted in Julian Ozanne, 'Palestinian aid programme has been a failure', *Financial Times*, 22 November 1994.
8. Joe Stork and Beshara Doumani, 'After Oslo', *Middle East Report*, January–February 1994.
9. Bashir Barghouti, 'Rejected Israeli threats and the required Palestinian reexamination', *Palestine Report*, 4 September 1994.
10. Ehud Ya'ari, 'Can Arafat govern?'.
11. Raji Sourani, in a speech at the International Colloquium on Human Rights, Gaza, 9–12 September 1994.
12. Farid Jarbou was arrested by the Palestinian police on 26 June 1994 and declared dead on 6 July 1994. His father said that his son's body was 'covered with signs of violence'.
13. For an interesting Israeli analysis of these developments, see Nadar Ha'etzni in *Ma'ariv*, 22 June and 2 September 1994 (translated in *Foreign Broadcast Information Service*, 25 July and 7 September 1994).
14. Lamis Andoni, 'Islamist group signals shift'.
15. Steve Roden and Bill Hutman, 'Order in Jericho', *Jerusalem Post Magazine*, 19 May 1995, pp. 10–15.
16. Reported in Uzi Benziman, *Ha'aretz*, 2 December 1994.
17. Lamis Andoni, 'Arafat falls back on Fatah', *Middle East International*, 2 December 1994.
18. Quoted in *Yediot Aharonot*, 7 September 1993.
19. Tamari, 'The critics'.
20. Bashir Barghouti, 'There is no meaning in elections without a legislative assembly', *Al-Tali'a*, 16 June 1994.
21. Jarrar, 'The Islamist movement'.
22. Raji Sourani speech, September 1994.
23. Isabel Kershner, 'A smooth operation?', *Jerusalem Report*, 11 August 1994.
24. Lamis Andoni, 'Arafat seeks new role for Fatah', *Middle East International*, 27 May 1994.
25. Marwan Barghouti, 'Arafat and the opposition'.
26. Andoni, 'Arafat seeks new role'.

27. Ghassan Khatib, 'Elections and saving what can be saved', *Al Quds*, 30 September 1994.
28. Azmi Bishara, 'Can there be legitimate representation in the elections under the shadow of autonomy?', *Al-Hayat*, 6–7 October 1994.

Epilogue

1. Eqbal Ahmad, 'Pioneering in the nuclear age: an essay on Israel and the Palestinians', *Race & Class* Spring 1984.
2. The countries which voted against were Israel, the US and Dominica.
3. John Pilger, 'Children of Palestine', *Distant Voices* (New York: Vintage, 1992).
4. Noam Chomsky, *World Orders, Old and New* (London: Pluto Press, 1994) p. 252.
5. Quoted in Stork and Doumani, 'After Oslo'.
6. Naseer Aruri, 'The crisis in Palestinian politics', *Middle East International*, 21 January 1994.
7. Israel Shahak, 'Settling the West Bank and Israeli domestic politics', *Shahak Report* No. 149, 29 January 1995.
8. Meron Benvenisti, *Ha'aretz*, 22 December 1994.
9. Jules Kagian, 'Forced to the margins', *Middle East International*, 7 October 1994.
10. Thus, since May 1994, the US has been urging UNRWA, the UN agency responsible for the welfare of the Palestinian refugees, to 'positively address the question of its own demise'. See Graham Usher, 'Burying the Palestinians', *Middle East International*, 6 January 1995.
11. 'Massive arrest campaign in Gaza Strip', Gaza Centre for Rights and Law, press release, 9 February 1995.
12. 'Appeal to Chairman Arafat to reverse decree establishing a state security court', Gaza Centre for Rights and Law, press release, 12 February 1995.
13. I owe the phrase to Lamis Andoni.
14. Ghassan Khatib, 'Was the Cairo Agreement an inevitable fate?', *Palestine Report*, 20 June 1994.
15. See Chapter 4.
16. Abed, 'Developing the Palestinian economy'.
17. Aruri, 'The crisis in Palestinian politics'.
18. Bishara, 'Can there be legitimate representation in the elections'.
19. On 5 January 1995, Haidar Abd al-Shafi established the Movement for Palestinian Democracy, open to 'all individuals who believe and adhere to democracy and work to disseminate democratic values and practices in Palestinian society'. See Lamis Andoni, 'Palestinian movement for democracy takes shape', *Jordan Times*, 15 January 1995.
20. Haidar Abd al-Shafi, *News from Within*, 5 August 1993.

Appendix 1. Declaration of Principles on Interim Self-Government Arrangements ('Oslo Agreement')

The Government of the State of Israel and the PLO team (in the Jordanian–Palestinian delegation to the Middle East Peace Conference) (the "Palestinian Delegation"), representing the Palestinian people, agree that it is time to put an end to decades of confrontation and conflict, recognize their mutual legitimate and political rights, and strive to live in peaceful coexistence and mutual dignity and security and achieve a just, lasting and comprehensive peace settlement and historic reconciliation through the agreed political process. Accordingly, the two sides agree to the following principles:

Article I
AIM OF THE NEGOTIATIONS
The aim of the Israeli–Palestinian negotiations within the current Middle East peace process is, among other things, to establish a Palestinian Interim Self-Government Authority, the elected Council (the "Council"), for the Palestinian people in the West Bank and the Gaza Strip, for a transitional period not exceeding five years, leading to a permanent settlement based on Security Council Resolutions 242 and 338.

It is understood that the interim arrangements are an integral part of the whole peace process and that the negotiations on the permanent status will lead to the implementation of Security Council Resolutions 242 and 338.

Article II
FRAMEWORK FOR THE INTERIM PERIOD
The agreed framework for the interim period is set forth in this Declaration of Principles.

Article III
ELECTIONS
1. In order that the Palestinian people in the West Bank and Gaza Strip may govern themselves according to democratic principles, direct, free

93

and general political elections will be held for the Council under agreed supervision and international observation, while the Palestinian police will ensure public order.

2. An agreement will be concluded on the exact mode and conditions of the elections in accordance with the protocol attached as Annex I, with the goal of holding the elections not later than nine months after the entry into force of this Declaration of Principles.

3. These elections will constitute a significant interim preparatory step toward the realization of the legitimate rights of the Palestinian people and their just requirements.

Article IV
JURISDICTION
Jurisdiction of the Council will cover West Bank and Gaza Strip territory, except for issues that will be negotiated in the permanent status negotiations. The two sides view the West Bank and the Gaza Strip as a single territorial unit, whose integrity will be preserved during the interim period.

Article V
TRANSITIONAL PERIOD AND PERMANENT STATUS NEGOTIATIONS
1. The five-year transitional period will begin upon the withdrawal from the Gaza Strip and Jericho area.

2. Permanent status negotiations will commence as soon as possible, but not later than the beginning of the third year of the interim period, between the Government of Israel and the Palestinian people's representatives.

3. It is understood that these negotiations shall cover remaining issues, including: Jerusalem, refugees, settlements, security arrangements, borders, relations and cooperation with other neighbors, and other issues of common interest.

4. The two parties agree that the outcome of the permanent status negotiations should not be prejudiced or preempted by agreements reached for the interim period.

Article VI
PREPARATORY TRANSFER OF POWERS AND RESPONSIBILITIES
1. Upon the entry into force of this Declaration of Principles and the withdrawal from the Gaza Strip and the Jericho area, a transfer of authority from the Israeli military government and its Civil Administration to the authorised Palestinians for this task, as detailed herein, will commence. This transfer of authority will be of a preparatory nature until the inauguration of the Council.

2. Immediately after the entry into force of this Declaration of Principles and the withdrawal from the Gaza Strip and Jericho area, with the view to promoting economic development in the West Bank and Gaza Strip,

authority will be transferred to the Palestinians on the following spheres: education and culture, health, social welfare, direct taxation, and tourism. The Palestinian side will commence in building the Palestinian police force, as agreed upon. Pending the inauguration of the Council, the two parties may negotiate the transfer of additional powers and responsibilities, as agreed upon.

Article VII
INTERIM AGREEMENT
1. The Israeli and Palestinian delegations will negotiate an agreement on the interim period (the "Interim Agreement").
2. The Interim Agreement shall specify, among other things, the structure of the Council, the number of its members, and the transfer of powers and responsibilities from the Israeli military government and its Civil Administration to the Council. The Interim Agreement shall also specify the Council's executive authority, legislative authority in accordance with Article IX below, and the independent Palestinian judicial organs.
3. The Interim Agreement shall include arrangements, to be implemented upon the inauguration of the Council, for the assumption by the Council of all of the powers and responsibilities transferred previously in accordance with Article VI above.
4. In order to enable the Council to promote economic growth, upon its inauguration, the Council will establish, among other things, a Palestinian Electricity Authority, a Gaza Sea Port Authority, a Palestinian Development Bank, a Palestinian Export Promotion Board, a Palestinian Environmental Authority, a Palestinian Land Authority and a Palestinian Water Administration Authority, and any other Authorities agreed upon, in accordance with the Interim Agreement that will specify their powers and responsibilities.
5. After the inauguration of the Council, the Civil Administration will be dissolved, and the Israeli military government will be withdrawn.

Article VIII
PUBLIC ORDER AND SECURITY
In order to guarantee public order and internal security for the Palestinians of the West Bank and the Gaza Strip, the Council will establish a strong police force, while Israel will continue to carry the responsibility for defending against external threats, as well as the responsibility for overall security of Israelis for the purpose of safeguarding their internal security and public order.

Article IX
LAWS AND MILITARY ORDERS
1. The Council will be empowered to legislate, in accordance with the Interim Agreement, within all authorities transferred to it.

2. Both parties will review jointly laws and military orders presently in force in remaining spheres.

Article X
JOINT ISRAELI–PALESTINIAN LIAISON COMMITTEE
In order to provide for a smooth implementation of this Declaration of Principles and any subsequent agreements pertaining to the interim period, upon the entry into force of this Declaration of Principles, a Joint Israeli–Palestinian Liaison Committee will be established in order to deal with issues requiring coordination, other issues of common interest, and disputes.

Article XI
ISRAELI–PALESTINIAN COOPERATION IN ECONOMIC FIELDS
Recognizing the mutual benefit of cooperation in promoting the development of the West Bank, the Gaza Strip and Israel, upon the entry into force of this Declaration of Principles, an Israeli–Palestinian Economic Cooperation Committee will be established in order to develop and implement in a cooperative manner the programs identified in the protocols attached as Annex III and Annex IV.

Article XII
LIAISON AND COOPERATION WITH JORDAN AND EGYPT
The two parties will invite the Governments of Jordan and Egypt to participate in establishing further liaison and cooperation arrangements between the Government of Israel and the Palestinian representatives, on the one hand, and the Governments of Jordan and Egypt, on the other hand, to promote cooperation between them. These arrangements will include the constitution of a Continuing Committee that will decide by agreement on the modalities of admission of persons displaced from the West Bank and Gaza Strip in 1967, together with necessary measures to prevent disruption and disorder. Other matters of common concern will be dealt with by this Committee.

Article XIII
REDEPLOYMENT OF ISRAELI FORCES
1. After the entry into force of this Declaration of Principles, and not later than the eve of elections for the Council, a redeployment of Israeli military forces in the West Bank and the Gaza Strip will take place, in addition to withdrawal of Israeli forces carried out in accordance with Article XIV.
2. In redeploying its military forces, Israel will be guided by the principle that its military forces should be redeployed outside populated areas.
3. Further redeployments to specified locations will be gradually implemented commensurate with the assumption of responsibility for public

order and internal security by the Palestinian police force pursuant to Article VIII above.

Article XIV
ISRAELI WITHDRAWAL FROM THE GAZA STRIP AND JERICHO AREA
Israel will withdraw from the Gaza Strip and Jericho area, as detailed in the protocol attached as Annex II.

Article XV
RESOLUTION OF DISPUTES
1. Disputes arising out of the application or interpretation of this Declaration of Principles or any subsequent agreements pertaining to the interim period, shall be resolved by negotiations through the Joint Liaison Committee to be established pursuant to Article X above.
2. Disputes which cannot be settled by negotiations may be resolved by a mechanism of conciliation to be agreed upon by the parties.
3. The parties may agree to submit to arbitration disputes relating to the interim period, which cannot be settled through conciliation. To this end, upon the agreement of both parties, the parties will establish an Arbitration Committee.

Article XVI
ISRAELI–PALESTINIAN COOPERATION CONCERNING REGIONAL PROGRAMS
Both parties view the multilateral working groups as an appropriate instrument for promoting a "Marshall Plan", the regional programs and other programs, including special programs for the West Bank and Gaza Strip, as indicated in the protocol attached as Annex IV.

Article XVII
MISCELLANEOUS PROVISIONS
1. This Declaration of Principles will enter into force one month after its signing.
2. All protocols annexed to this Declaration of Principles and Agreed Minutes pertaining thereto shall be regarded as an integral part hereof.

Done at Washington, D.C., this thirteenth day of September, 1993. For the Government of Israel. For the PLO. Witnessed By: The United States of America, The Russian Federation.

Annex I
PROTOCOL ON THE MODE AND CONDITIONS OF ELECTIONS
1. Palestinians of Jerusalem who live there will have the right to participate in the election process, according to an agreement between the two sides.

2. In addition, the election agreement should cover, among other things, the following issues:

a. the system of elections;

b. the mode of the agreed supervision and international observation and their personal composition; and

c. rules and regulations regarding election campaign, including agreed arrangements for the organizing of mass media, and the possibility of licensing a broadcasting and TV station.

3. The future status of displaced Palestinians who were registered on 4th June 1967 will not be prejudiced because they are unable to participate in the election process due to practical reasons.

Annex II
PROTOCOL ON WITHDRAWAL OF ISRAELI FORCES FROM THE GAZA STRIP AND JERICHO AREA

1. The two sides will conclude and sign within two months from the date of entry into force of this Declaration of Principles, an agreement on the withdrawal of Israeli military forces from the Gaza Strip and Jericho area. This agreement will include comprehensive arrangements to apply in the Gaza Strip and the Jericho area subsequent to the Israeli withdrawal.

2. Israel will implement an accelerated and scheduled withdrawal of Israeli military forces from the Gaza Strip and Jericho area, beginning immediately with the signing of the agreement on the Gaza Strip and Jericho area and to be completed within a period not exceeding four months after the signing of this agreement.

3. The above agreement will include, among other things:

a. Arrangements for a smooth and peaceful transfer of authority from the Israeli military government and its Civil Administration to the Palestinian representatives.

b. Structure, powers and responsibilities of the Palestinian authority in these areas, except: external security, settlements, Israelis, foreign relations, and other mutually agreed matters.

c. Arrangements for the assumption of internal security and public order by the Palestinian police force consisting of police officers recruited locally and from abroad holding Jordanian passports and Palestinian documents issued by Egypt. Those who will participate in the Palestinian police force coming from abroad should be trained as police and police officers.

d. A temporary international or foreign presence, as agreed upon.

e. Establishment of a joint Palestinian–Israeli Coordination and Cooperation Committee for mutual security purposes.

f. An economic development and stabilization program, including the establishment of an Emergency Fund, to encourage foreign investment, and financial and economic support. Both sides will coordinate and cooperate jointly and unilaterally with regional and international parties to support these aims.

g. Arrangements for a safe passage for persons and transportation between the Gaza Strip and Jericho area.

4. The above agreement will include arrangements for coordination between both parties regarding passages:

a. Gaza–Egypt; and

b. Jericho–Jordan.

5. The offices responsible for carrying out the powers and responsibilities of the Palestinian authority under this Annex II and Article VI of the Declaration of Principles will be located in the Gaza Strip and in the Jericho area pending the inauguration of the Council.

6. Other than these agreed arrangements, the status of the Gaza Strip and Jericho area will continue to be an integral part of the West Bank and Gaza Strip, and will not be changed in the interim period.

Annex III
PROTOCOL ON ISRAELI–PALESTINIAN COOPERATION IN ECONOMIC AND DEVELOPMENT PROGRAMS

The two sides agree to establish an Israeli–Palestinian continuing Committee for Economic Cooperation, focusing, among other things, on the following:

1. Cooperation in the field of water, including a Water Development Program prepared by experts from both sides, which will also specify the mode of cooperation in the management of water resources in the West Bank and Gaza Strip, and will include proposals for studies and plans on water rights of each party, as well as on the equitable utilization of joint water resources for implementation in and beyond the interim period.

2. Cooperation in the field of electricity, including an Electricity Development Program, which will also specify the mode of cooperation for the production, maintenance, purchase and sale of electricity resources.

3. Cooperation in the field of energy, including an Energy Development Program, which will provide for the exploitation of oil and gas for industrial purposes, particularly in the Gaza Strip and in the Negev, and will encourage further joint exploitation of other energy resources. This Program may also provide for the construction of a Petrochemical industrial complex in the Gaza Strip and the construction of oil and gas pipelines.

4. Cooperation in the field of finance, including a Financial Development and Action Program for the encouragement of international investment in the West Bank and the Gaza Strip, and in Israel, as well as the establishment of a Palestinian Development Bank.

5. Cooperation in the field of transport and communications, including a Program, which will define guidelines for the establishment of a Gaza Sea Port Area, and will provide for the establishing of transport and com-

munications lines to and from the West Bank and the Gaza Strip to Israel and to other countries. In addition, this Program will provide for carrying out the necessary construction of roads, railways, communications lines, etc.

6. Cooperation in the field of trade, including studies, and Trade Promotion Programs, which will encourage local, regional and inter-regional trade, as well as a feasibility study of creating free trade zones in the Gaza Strip and in Israel, mutual access to these zones, and cooperation in other areas related to trade and commerce.

7. Cooperation in the field of industry, including Industrial Development Programs, which will provide for the establishment of joint Israeli–Palestinian Industrial Research and Development Centers, will promote Palestinian–Israeli joint ventures, and provide guidelines for cooperation in the textile, food, pharmaceutical, electronics, diamonds, computer and science-based industries.

8. A program for cooperation in, and regulation of, labor relations and cooperation in social welfare issues.

9. A Human Resources Development and Cooperation Plan, providing for joint Israeli–Palestinian workshops and seminars, and for the establishment of joint vocational training centers, research institutes and data banks.

10. An Environmental Protection Plan, providing for joint and/or coordinated measures in this sphere.

11. A program for developing coordination and cooperation in the field of communication and media.

12. Any other programs of mutual interest.

Annex IV
PROTOCOL ON ISRAELI–PALESTINIAN COOPERATION
CONCERNING REGIONAL DEVELOPMENT PROGRAMS

1. The two sides will cooperate in the context of the multilateral peace efforts in promoting a Development Program for the region, including the West Bank and the Gaza Strip, to be initiated by the G-7. The parties will request the G-7 to seek the participation in this program of other interested states, such as members of the Organisation for Economic Cooperation and Development, regional Arab states and institutions, as well as members of the private sector.

2. The Development Program will consist of two elements:
   a. an Economic Development Program for the West Bank and the Gaza Strip.
   b. a Regional Economic Development Program.

A. The Economic Development Program for the West Bank and the Gaza strip will consist of the following elements:
   (1) A Social Rehabilitation Program, including a Housing and Construction Program.

(2) A Small and Medium Business Development Plan.

(3) An Infrastructure Development Program (water, electricity, transportation and communications, etc.).

(4) A Human Resources Plan.

(5) Other programs.

B. The Regional Economic Development Program may consist of the following elements:

(1) The establishment of a Middle East Development Fund, as a first step, and a Middle East Development Bank, as a second step.

(2) The development of a joint Israeli–Palestinian–Jordanian Plan for coordinated exploitation of the Dead Sea area.

(3) The Mediterranean Sea (Gaza) – Dead Sea Canal.

(4) Regional Desalinization and other water development projects.

(5) A regional plan for agricultural development, including a coordinated regional effort for the prevention of desertification.

(6) Interconnection of electricity grids.

(7) Regional cooperation for the transfer, distribution and industrial exploitation of gas, oil and other energy resources.

(8) A Regional Tourism, Transportation and Telecommunications Development Plan.

(9) Regional cooperation in other spheres.

3. The two sides will encourage the multilateral working groups, and will coordinate towards their success. The two parties will encourage intersessional activities, as well as pre-feasibility and feasibility studies, within the various multilateral working groups.

AGREED MINUTES TO THE DECLARATION OF PRINCIPLES ON INTERIM SELF-GOVERNMENT ARRANGEMENTS

A. GENERAL UNDERSTANDINGS AND AGREEMENTS

Any powers and responsibilities transferred to the Palestinians pursuant to the Declaration of Principles prior to the inauguration of the Council will be subject to the same principles pertaining to Article IV, as set out in these Agreed Minutes below.

B. SPECIFIC UNDERSTANDINGS AND AGREEMENTS

Article IV

It is understood that:

1. Jurisdiction of the Council will cover West Bank and Gaza Strip territory, except for issues that will be negotiated in the permanent status negotiations: Jerusalem, settlements, military locations, and Israelis.

2. The Council's jurisdiction will apply with regard to the agreed powers, responsibilities, spheres and authorities transferred to it.

Article VI (2)
It is agreed that the transfer of authority will be as follows:
1. The Palestinian side will inform the Israeli side of the names of the authorised Palestinians who will assume the powers, authorities and responsibilities that will be transferred to the Palestinians according to the Declaration of Principles in the following fields: education and culture, health, social welfare, direct taxation, tourism, and any other authorities agreed upon.
2. It is understood that the rights and obligations of these offices will not be affected.
3. Each of the spheres described above will continue to enjoy existing budgetary allocations in accordance with arrangements to be mutually agreed upon. These arrangements also will provide for the necessary adjustments required in order to take into account the taxes collected by the direct taxation office.
4. Upon the execution of the Declaration of Principles, the Israeli and Palestinian delegations will immediately commence negotiations on a detailed plan for the transfer of authority on the above offices in accordance with the above understandings.

Article VII (2)
The Interim Agreement will also include arrangements for coordination and cooperation.

Article VII (5)
The withdrawal of the military government will not prevent Israel from exercising the powers and responsibilities not transferred to the Council.

Article VIII
It is understood that the Interim Agreement will include arrangements for cooperation and coordination between the two parties in this regard. It is also agreed that the transfer of powers and responsibilities to the Palestinian police will be accomplished in a phased manner, as agreed in the Interim Agreement.

Article X
It is agreed that, upon the entry into force of the Declaration of Principles, the Israeli and Palestinian delegations will exchange the names of the individuals designated by them as members of the Joint Israeli–Palestinian Liaison Committee.
It is further agreed that each side will have an equal number of members in the Joint Committee. The Joint Committee will reach decisions by agreement. The Joint Committee may add other technicians and experts, as necessary. The Joint Committee will decide on the frequency and place or places of its meetings.

Annex II
It is understood that, subsequent to the Israeli withdrawal, Israel will continue to be responsible for external security, and for internal security and public order of settlements and Israelis. Israeli military forces and civilians may continue to use roads freely within the Gaza Strip and the Jericho area.

Done at Washington, D.C., this thirteenth day of September, 1993. For the Government of Israel. For the PLO. Witnessed By: The United States of America, The Russian Federation.

Appendix 2. The Israel–PLO Agreement on the Gaza Strip and the Jericho Area ('Cairo Agreement')

The Government of the State of Israel and the Palestine Liberation Organization (hereinafter "the PLO"), the representative of the Palestinian people;

PREAMBLE
WITHIN the framework of the Middle East peace process initiated at Madrid in October 1991;
REAFFIRMING their determination to live in peaceful coexistence, mutual dignity and security, while recognizing their mutual legitimate and political rights;
REAFFIRMING their desire to achieve a just, lasting and comprehensive peace settlement through the agreed political process;
REAFFIRMING their adherence to the mutual recognition and commitments expressed in the letters dated September 9, 1993, signed by and exchanged between the Prime Minister of Israel and the Chairman of the PLO;
REAFFIRMING their understanding that the interim self-government arrangements, including the arrangements to apply in the Gaza Strip and the Jericho Area contained in this Agreement, are an integral part of the whole peace process and that the negotiations on the permanent status will lead to the implementation of Security Council Resolutions 242 and 338;
DESIROUS of putting into effect the Declaration of Principles on Interim Self-Government Arrangements signed at Washington, D.C. on September 13, 1993, and the Agreed Minutes thereto (hereinafter "the Declaration of Principles"), and in particular the Protocol on withdrawal of Israeli forces from the Gaza Strip and the Jericho Area;
HEREBY AGREE to the following arrangements regarding the Gaza Strip and the Jericho Area:

Article I
Definitions
For the purpose of this Agreement:
a. the Gaza Strip and the Jericho Area are delineated on map Nos. 1 and 2 attached to this Agreement;*
b. "the Settlements" means the Gush Katif and Erez settlement areas, as well as the other settlements in the Gaza Strip, as shown on attached map No. 1;
c. "the Military Installation Area" means the Israeli military installation area along the Egyptian border in the Gaza Strip, as shown on map No. 1; and
d. the term "Israelis" shall also include Israeli statutory agencies and corporations registered in Israel.

Article II
Scheduled Withdrawal of Israeli Military Forces
1. Israel shall implement an accelerated and scheduled withdrawal of Israeli military forces from the Gaza Strip and from the Jericho Area to begin immediately with the signing of this Agreement. Israel shall complete such withdrawal within three weeks from this date.
2. Subject to the arrangements included in the Protocol Concerning Withdrawal of Israeli Military Forces and Security Arrangements attached as Annex I, the Israeli withdrawal shall include evacuating all military bases and other fixed installations to be handed over to the Palestinian Police, to be established pursuant to Article IX below (hereinafter "the Palestinian Police").
3. In order to carry out Israel's responsibility for external security and for internal security and public order of Settlements and Israelis, Israel shall, concurrently with the withdrawal, redeploy its remaining military forces to the Settlements and the Military Installation Area, in accordance with the provisions of this Agreement. Subject to the provisions of this Agreement, this redeployment shall constitute full implementation of Article XIII of the Declaration of Principles with regard to the Gaza Strip and the Jericho Area only.
4. For the purposes of this Agreement, "Israeli military forces" may include Israel police and other Israeli security forces.
5. Israelis, including Israeli military forces, may continue to use roads freely within the Gaza Strip and the Jericho Area. Palestinians may use public roads crossing the Settlements freely, as provided for in Annex I.
6. The Palestinian Police shall be deployed and shall assume responsibility for public order and internal security of Palestinians in accordance with this Agreement and Annex I.

---

* Maps not reproduced in this volume

Article III
Transfer of Authority
1. Israel shall transfer authority as specified in this Agreement from the Israeli military government and its Civil Administration to the Palestinian Authority, hereby established, in accordance with Article V of this Agreement, except for the authority that Israel shall continue to exercise as specified in this Agreement.
2. As regards the transfer and assumption of authority in civil spheres, powers and responsibilities shall be transferred and assumed as set out in the Protocol Concerning Civil Affairs attached as Annex II.
3. Arrangements for a smooth and peaceful transfer of the agreed powers and responsibilities are set out in Annex II.
4. Upon the completion of the Israeli withdrawal and the transfer of powers and responsibilities as detailed in paragraphs 1 and 2 above and in Annex II, the Civil Administration in the Gaza Strip and the Jericho Area will be dissolved and the Israeli military government will be withdrawn. The withdrawal of the military government shall not prevent it from continuing to exercise the powers and responsibilities specified in this Agreement.
5. A Joint Civil Affairs Coordination and Cooperation Committee (hereinafter "the CAC") and two Joint Regional Civil Affairs Subcommittees for the Gaza Strip and the Jericho Area respectively shall be established in order to provide for coordination and cooperation in civil affairs between the Palestinian Authority and Israel, as detailed in Annex II.
6. The offices of the Palestinian Authority shall be located in the Gaza Strip and the Jericho Area pending the inauguration of the Council to be elected pursuant to the Declaration of Principles.

Article IV
Structure and Composition of the Palestinian Authority
1. The Palestinian Authority will consist of one body of 24 members which shall carry out and be responsible for all the legislative and executive powers and responsibilities transferred to it under this Agreement, in accordance with this Article, and shall be responsible for the exercise of judicial functions in accordance with Article VI, subparagraph 1.b. of this Agreement.
2. The Palestinian Authority shall administer the departments transferred to it and may establish, within its jurisdiction, other departments and subordinate administrative units as necessary for the fulfillment of its responsibilities. It shall determine its own internal procedures.
3. The PLO shall inform the Government of Israel of the names of the members of the Palestinian Authority and any change of members. Changes in the membership of the Palestinian Authority will take effect upon an exchange of letters between the PLO and the Government of Israel.

4. Each member of the Palestinian Authority shall enter into office upon undertaking to act in accordance with this Agreement.

Article V
Jurisdiction
1. The authority of the Palestinian Authority encompasses all matters that fall within its territorial, functional and personal jurisdiction, as follows:

a. The territorial jurisdiction covers the Gaza Strip and the Jericho Area territory, as defined in Article I, except for Settlements and the Military Installation Area.
Territorial jurisdiction shall include land, subsoil and territorial waters, in accordance with the provisions of this Agreement.

b. The functional jurisdiction encompasses all powers and responsibilities as specified in this Agreement. This jurisdiction does not include foreign relations, internal security and public order of Settlements and the Military Installation Area and Israelis, and external security.

c. The personal jurisdiction extends to all persons within the territorial jurisdiction referred to above, except for Israelis, unless otherwise provided in this Agreement.

2. The Palestinian Authority has, within its authority, legislative, executive and judicial powers and responsibilities, as provided for in this Agreement.

3. a. Israel has authority over the Settlements, the Military Installation Area, Israelis, external security, internal security and public order of Settlements, the Military Installation Area and Israelis, and those agreed powers and responsibilities specified in this Agreement.

b. Israel shall exercise its authority through its military government, which, for that end, shall continue to have the necessary legislative, judicial and executive powers and responsibilities, in accordance with international law. This provision shall not derogate from Israel's applicable legislation over Israelis in personam.

4. The exercise of authority with regard to the electromagnetic sphere and airspace shall be in accordance with the provisions of this Agreement.

5. The provisions of this Article are subject to the specific legal arrangements detailed in the Protocol Concerning Legal Matters attached as Annex III. Israel and the Palestinian Authority may negotiate further legal arrangements.

6. Israel and the Palestinian Authority shall cooperate on matters of legal assistance in criminal and civil matters through the legal subcommittee of the CAC.

Article VI
Powers and Responsibilities of the Palestinian Authority
1. Subject to the provisions of this Agreement, the Palestinian Authority, within its jurisdiction:

a. has legislative powers as set out in Article VII of this Agreement, as well as executive powers;

b. will administer justice through an independent judiciary;

c. will have, inter alia, power to formulate policies, supervise their implementation, employ staff, establish departments, authorities and institutions, sue and be sued and conclude contracts; and

d. will have, inter alia, the power to keep and administer registers and records of the population, and issue certificates, licenses and documents.

2. a. In accordance with the Declaration of Principles, the Palestinian Authority will not have powers and responsibilities in the sphere of foreign relations, which sphere includes the establishment abroad of embassies, consulates or other types of foreign missions and posts or permitting their establishment in the Gaza Strip or the Jericho Area, the appointment of or admission of diplomatic and consular staff, and the exercise of diplomatic functions.

b. Notwithstanding the provisions of this paragraph, the PLO may conduct negotiations and sign agreements with states or international organizations for the benefit of the Palestinian Authority in the following cases only:

(1) economic agreements, as specifically provided in Annex IV of this Agreement;

(2) agreements with donor countries for the purpose of implementing arrangements for the provision of assistance to the Palestinian Authority;

(3) agreements for the purpose of implementing the regional development plans detailed in Annex IV of the Declaration of Principles or in agreements entered into in the framework of the multilateral negotiations; and

(4) cultural, scientific and educational agreements.

c. Dealings between the Palestinian Authority and representatives of foreign states and international organizations, as well as the establishment in the Gaza Strip and the Jericho Area of representative offices other than those described in subparagraph 2.a. above, for the purpose of implementing the agreements referred to in subparagraph 2.b. above, shall not be considered foreign relations.

Article VII

Legislative Powers of the Palestinian Authority

1. The Palestinian Authority will have the power, within its jurisdiction, to promulgate legislation, including basic laws, laws, regulations and other legislative acts.

2. Legislation promulgated by the Palestinian Authority shall be consistent with the provisions of this Agreement.

3. Legislation promulgated by the Palestinian Authority shall be communicated to a legislation subcommittee to be established by the CAC

(hereinafter "the Legislation Subcommittee"). During a period of 30 days from the communication of the legislation, Israel may request that the Legislation Subcommittee decide whether such legislation exceeds the jurisdiction of the Palestinian Authority or is otherwise inconsistent with the provisions of this Agreement.

4. Upon receipt of the Israeli request, the Legislation Subcommittee shall decide, as an initial matter, on the entry into force of the legislation pending its decision on the merits of the matter.

5. If the Legislation Subcommittee is unable to reach a decision with regard to the entry into force of the legislation within 15 days, this issue will be referred to a board of review. This board of review shall be comprised of two judges, retired judges or senior jurists (hereinafter "Judges"), one from each side, to be appointed from a compiled list of three Judges proposed by each.

In order to expedite the proceedings before this board of review, the two most senior Judges, one from each side, shall develop written informal rules of procedure.

6. Legislation referred to the board of review shall enter into force only if the board of review decides that it does not deal with a security issue which falls under Israel's responsibility, that it does not seriously threaten other significant Israeli interests protected by this Agreement and that the entry into force of the legislation could not cause irreparable damage or harm.

7. The Legislation Subcommittee shall attempt to reach a decision on the merits of the matter within 30 days from the date of the Israeli request. If this Subcommittee is unable to reach such a decision within this period of 30 days, the matter shall be referred to the Joint Israeli–Palestinian Liaison Committee referred to in Article XV below (hereinafter "the Liaison Committee"). This Liaison Committee will deal with the matter immediately and will attempt to settle it within 30 days.

8. Where the legislation has not entered into force pursuant to paragraphs 5 or 7 above, this situation shall be maintained pending the decision of the Liaison Committee on the merits of the matter, unless it has decided otherwise.

9. Laws and military orders in effect in the Gaza Strip or the Jericho Area prior to the signing of this Agreement shall remain in force, unless amended or abrogated in accordance with this Agreement.

Article VIII
Arrangements for Security and Public Order

1. In order to guarantee public order and internal security for the Palestinians of the Gaza Strip and the Jericho Area, the Palestinian Authority shall establish a strong police force, as set out in Article IX below. Israel shall continue to carry the responsibility for defense against external threats, including the responsibility for protecting the Egyptian border and the Jordanian line, and for defense against external threats from the

sea and from the air, as well as the responsibility for overall security of Israelis and Settlements, for the purpose of safeguarding their internal security and public order, and will have all the powers to take the steps necessary to meet this responsibility.

2. Agreed security arrangements and coordination mechanisms are specified in Annex I.

3. A joint Coordination and Cooperation Committee for mutual security purposes (hereinafter "the JSC"), as well as three joint District Coordination and Cooperation Offices for the Gaza district, the Khan Yunis district and the Jericho district respectively (hereinafter "the DCOs") are hereby established as provided for in Annex I.

4. The security arrangements provided for in this Agreement and in Annex I may be reviewed at the request of either Party and may be amended by mutual agreement of the Parties. Specific review arrangements are included in Annex I.

Article IX
The Palestinian Directorate of Police Force

1. The Palestinian Authority shall establish a strong police force, the Palestinian Directorate of Police Force (hereinafter "the Palestinian Police"). The duties, functions, structure, deployment and composition of the Palestinian Police, together with provisions regarding its equipment and operation, are set out in Annex I, Article III. Rules of conduct governing the activities of the Palestinian Police are set out in Annex I, Article VIII.

2. Except for the Palestinian Police referred to in this Article and the Israeli military forces, no other armed forces shall be established or operate in the Gaza Strip or the Jericho Area.

3. Except for the arms, ammunition and equipment of the Palestinian Police described in Annex I, Article III, and those of the Israeli military forces, no organization or individual in the Gaza Strip and the Jericho Area shall manufacture, sell, acquire, possess, import or otherwise introduce into the Gaza Strip or the Jericho Area any firearms, ammunition, weapons, explosives, gunpowder or any related equipment, unless otherwise provided for in Annex I.

Article X
Passages

Arrangements for coordination between Israel and the Palestinian Authority regarding the Gaza–Egypt and Jericho–Jordan passages, as well as any other agreed international crossings, are set out in Annex I, Article X.

Article XI
Safe Passage between the Gaza Strip and the Jericho Area

Arrangements for safe passage of persons and transportation between the Gaza Strip and the Jericho Area are set out in Annex I, Article IX.

Article XII
Relations Between Israel and the Palestinian Authority
1. Israel and the Palestinian Authority shall seek to foster mutual under-standing and tolerance and shall accordingly abstain from incitement, including hostile propaganda, against each other and, without derogating from the principle of freedom of expression, shall take legal measures to prevent such incitement by any organizations, groups or individuals within their jurisdiction.
2. Without derogating from the other provisions of this Agreement, Israel and the Palestinian Authority shall cooperate in combatting criminal activity which may affect both sides, including offenses related to trafficking in illegal drugs and psychotropic substances, smuggling, and offenses against property, including offenses related to vehicles.

Article XIII
Economic Relations
The economic relations between the two sides are set out in the Protocol on Economic Relations signed in Paris on April 29, 1994 and the Appendices thereto, certified copies of which are attached as Annex IV, and will be governed by the relevant provisions of this Agreement and its Annexes.

Article XIV
Human Rights and the Rule of Law
Israel and the Palestinian Authority shall exercise their powers and responsibilities pursuant to this Agreement with due regard to inter-nationally-accepted norms and principles of human rights and the rule of law.

Article XV
The Joint Israeli–Palestinian Liaison Committee
1. The Liaison Committee established pursuant to Article X of the Dec-laration of Principles shall ensure the smooth implementation of this Agreement. It shall deal with issues requiring coordination, other issues of common interest and disputes.
2. The Liaison Committee shall be composed of an equal number of members from each Party. It may add other technicians and experts as necessary.
3. The Liaison Committee shall adopt its rules of procedure, including the frequency and place or places of its meetings.
4. The Liaison Committee shall reach its decisions by Agreement.

Article XVI
Liaison and Cooperation with Jordan and Egypt
1. Pursuant to Article XII of the Declaration of Principles, the two Parties shall invite the Governments of Jordan and Egypt to participate in estab-

lishing further liaison and cooperation arrangements between the
Government of Israel and the Palestinian representatives on the one hand,
and the Governments of Jordan and Egypt on the other hand, to promote
cooperation between them. These arrangements shall include the constitution of a Continuing Committee.
2. The Continuing Committee shall decide by agreement on the modalities
of admission of persons displaced from the West Bank and the Gaza Strip
in 1967, together with necessary measures to prevent disruption and
disorder.
3. The Continuing Committee shall deal with other matters of common
concern.

Article XVII
Settlement of Differences and Disputes
Any difference relating to the application of this Agreement shall be
referred to the appropriate coordination and cooperation mechanism
established under this Agreement. The provisions of Article XV of the
Declaration of Principles shall apply to any such difference which is not
settled through the appropriate coordination and cooperation mechanism,
namely:
1. Disputes arising out of the application or interpretation of this
Agreement or any subsequent agreements pertaining to the interim
period shall be settled by negotiations through the Liaison Committee.
2. Disputes which cannot be settled by negotiations may be settled by
a mechanism of conciliation to be agreed between the Parties.
3. The Parties may agree to submit to arbitration disputes relating to the
interim period, which cannot be settled through conciliation. To this
end, upon the agreement of both Parties, the Parties will establish an
Arbitration Committee.

Article XVIII
Prevention of Hostile Acts
Both sides shall take all measures necessary in order to prevent acts of
terrorism, crime and hostilities directed against each other, against individuals falling under the other's authority and against their property,
and shall take legal measures against offenders. In addition, the Palestinian side shall take all measures necessary to prevent such hostile acts
directed against the Settlements, the infrastructure serving them and the
Military Installation Area, and the Israeli side shall take all measures
necessary to prevent such hostile acts emanating from the Settlements
and directed against Palestinians.

Article XIX
Missing Persons
The Palestinian Authority shall cooperate with Israel by providing all
necessary assistance in the conduct of searches by Israel within the Gaza

Strip and the Jericho Area for missing Israelis, as well as by providing information about missing Israelis. Israel shall cooperate with the Palestinian Authority in searching for, and providing necessary information about, missing Palestinians.

Article XX
Confidence Building Measures
With a view to creating a positive and supportive public atmosphere to accompany the implementation of this Agreement, and to establish a solid basis of mutual trust and good faith, both Parties agree to carry out confidence building measures as detailed herewith:

1. Upon the signing of this Agreement, Israel will release, or turn over, to the Palestinian Authority within a period of 5 weeks, about 5,000 Palestinian detainees and prisoners, residents of the West Bank and the Gaza Strip. Those released will be free to return to their homes anywhere in the West Bank or the Gaza Strip. Prisoners turned over to the Palestinian Authority shall be obliged to remain in the Gaza Strip or the Jericho Area for the remainder of their sentence.

2. After the signing of this Agreement, the two Parties shall continue to negotiate the release of additional Palestinian prisoners and detainees, building on agreed principles.

3. The implementation of the above measures will be subject to the fulfillment of the procedures determined by Israeli law for the release and transfer of detainees and prisoners.

4. With the assumption of Palestinian authority, the Palestinian side commits itself to solving the problem of those Palestinians who were in contact with the Israeli authorities. Until an agreed solution is found, the Palestinian side undertakes not to prosecute these Palestinians or to harm them in any way.

5. Palestinians from abroad whose entry into the Gaza Strip and the Jericho Area is approved pursuant to this Agreement, and to whom the provisions of this Article are applicable, will not be prosecuted for offenses committed prior to September 13, 1993.

Article XXI
Temporary International Presence
1. The Parties agree to a temporary international or foreign presence in the Gaza Strip and the Jericho Area (hereinafter "the TIP"), in accordance with the provisions of this Article.

2. The TIP shall consist of 400 qualified personnel, including observers, instructors and other experts, from 5 or 6 of the donor countries.

3. The two Parties shall request the donor countries to establish a special fund to provide finance for the TIP.

4. The TIP will function for a period of 6 months. The TIP may extend this period, or change the scope of its operation, with the agreement of the two Parties.

5. The TIP shall be stationed and operate within the following cities and villages: Gaza, Khan Yunis, Rafah, Deir El Ballah, Jabaliya, Absan, Beit Hanun and Jericho.

6. Israel and the Palestinian Authority shall agree on a special Protocol to implement this Article, with the goal of concluding negotiations with the donor countries contributing personnel within two months.

Article XXII
Rights, Liabilities and Obligations

1. a. The transfer of all powers and responsibilities to the Palestinian Authority, as detailed in Annex II, includes all related rights, liabilities and obligations arising with regard to acts or omissions which occurred prior to the transfer.

Israel will cease to bear any financial responsibility regarding such acts or omissions and the Palestinian Authority will bear all financial responsibility for these and for its own functioning.

b. Any financial claim made in this regard against Israel will be referred to the Palestinian Authority.

c. Israel shall provide the Palestinian Authority with the information it has regarding pending and anticipated claims brought before any court or tribunal against Israel in this regard.

d. Where legal proceedings are brought in respect of such a claim, Israel will notify the Palestinian Authority and enable it to participate in defending the claim and raise any arguments on its behalf.

e. In the event that an award is made against Israel by any court or tribunal in respect of such a claim, the Palestinian Authority shall reimburse Israel the full amount of the award.

f. Without prejudice to the above, where a court or tribunal hearing such a claim finds that liability rests solely with an employee or agent who acted beyond the scope of the powers assigned to him or her, unlawfully or with willful malfeasance, the Palestinian Authority shall not bear financial responsibility.

2. The transfer of authority in itself shall not affect rights, liabilities and obligations of any person or legal entity, in existence at the date of signing of this Agreement.

Article XXIII
Final Clauses

1. This Agreement shall enter into force on the date of its signing.

2. The arrangements established by this Agreement shall remain in force until and to the extent superseded by the Interim Agreement referred

to in the Declaration of Principles or any other agreement between the Parties.

3. The five-year interim period referred to in the Declaration of Principles commences on the date of the signing of this Agreement.

4. The Parties agree that, as long as this Agreement is in force, the security fence erected by Israel around the Gaza Strip shall remain in place and that the line demarcated by the fence, as shown on attached map No. 1, shall be authoritative only for the purpose of this Agreement.

5. Nothing in this Agreement shall prejudice or preempt the outcome of the negotiations on the interim agreement or on the permanent status to be conducted pursuant to the Declaration of Principles. Neither Party shall be deemed, by virtue of having entered into this Agreement, to have renounced or waived any of its existing rights, claims or positions.

6. The two Parties view the West Bank and the Gaza Strip as a single territorial unit, the integrity of which will be preserved during the interim period.

7. The Gaza Strip and the Jericho Area shall continue to be an integral part of the West Bank and the Gaza Strip, and their status shall not be changed for the period of this Agreement. Nothing in this Agreement shall be considered to change this status.

8. The Preamble to this Agreement, and all Annexes, Appendices and maps attached hereto, shall constitute an integral part hereof.

Done in Cairo this fourth day of May, 1994. For the Government of the State of Israel. For the PLO. Witnessed By: The United States of America, The Russian Federation, The Arab Republic of Egypt.

Appendix 3. Israel–PLO Protocol on Economic Relations ('Paris Protocol')

Between the Government of the State of Israel and the PLO, representing the Palestinian people;

PREAMBLE
The two parties view the economic domain as one of the cornerstones in their mutual relations with a view to enhance their interest in the achievement of a just, lasting and comprehensive peace. Both parties shall cooperate in this field in order to establish a sound economic base for these relations, which will be governed in various economic spheres by the principles of mutual respect of each other's economic interests, reciprocity, equity and fairness.

This protocol lays the groundwork for strengthening the economic base of the Palestinian side and for exercising its right of economic decision making in accordance with its own development plan and priorities. The two parties recognize each other's economic ties with other markets and the need to create a better economic environment for their peoples and individuals.

Article I
FRAMEWORK AND SCOPE OF THIS PROTOCOL
1. This protocol establishes the contractual agreement that will govern the economic relations between the two sides and will cover the West Bank and the Gaza Strip during the interim period.

The implementation will be according to the stages envisaged in the Declaration of Principles on Interim Self Government Arrangements signed in Washington D.C. on September 13, 1993 and the Agreed Minutes thereto. It will therefore begin in the Gaza Strip and the Jericho Area and at a later stage will also apply to the rest of the West Bank, according to the provisions of the Interim Agreement and to any other agreed arrangements between the two sides.
2. This Protocol, including its Appendices, will be incorporated into the Agreement on the Gaza Strip and the Jericho Area (in this Protocol – the Agreement), will be an integral part thereof and interpreted accord-

116

ingly. This paragraph refers solely to the Gaza Strip and the Jericho Area.

3. This Protocol will come into force upon the signing of the Agreement.

4. For the purpose of this Protocol, the term "Areas" means the areas under the jurisdiction of the Palestinian Authority, according to the provisions of the Agreement regarding territorial jurisdiction.

The Palestinian Jurisdiction in the subsequent agreements could cover areas, spheres or functions according to the Interim Agreement. Therefore, for the purpose of this Protocol, whenever applied, the term "Areas" shall be interpreted to mean functions and spheres also, as the case may be, with the necessary adjustments.

Article II
THE JOINT ECONOMIC COMMITTEE

1. Both parties will establish a Palestinian–Israeli Joint Economic Committee (hereinafter – the JEC) to follow up the implementation of this Protocol and to decide on problems related to it that may arise from time to time. Each side may request the review of any issue related to this Agreement by the JEC.

2. The JEC will serve as the continuing committee for economic cooperation envisaged in Annex III of the Declaration of Principles.

3. The JEC will consist of an equal number of members from each side and may establish sub-committees specified in this Protocol.

A sub-committee may include experts as necessary.

4. The JEC and its sub-committees shall reach their decisions by agreement and shall determine their rules of procedure and operation, including the frequency and place or places of their meetings.

Article III
IMPORT TAXES AND IMPORT POLICY

1. The import and customs policies of both sides will be according to the principles and arrangements detailed in this Article.

2. a. The Palestinian Authority will have all powers and responsibilities in the sphere of import and customs policy and procedures with regard to the following:

(1) Goods on List A1, attached hereto as Appendix I, locally-produced in Jordan and in Egypt particularly and in the other Arab countries, which the Palestinians will be able to import in quantities agreed upon by the two sides up to the Palestinian market needs as estimated according to para 3 below.

(2) Goods on List A2, attached hereto as Appendix II, from the Arab, Islamic and other countries, which the Palestinians will be able to import in quantities agreed upon by the two sides up to the Palestinian market needs as estimated according to para 3 below.

b. The import policy of the Palestinian Authority for Lists A1 and A2 will include independently determining and changing from time to time the rates of customs, purchase tax, levies, excises and other charges, the regulation of licensing requirements and procedures and of standard requirements. The valuation for custom purposes will be based upon the GATT 1994 agreement as of the date it will be introduced in Israel, and until then – on the Brussels Definition of Valuation (BDV) system. The classification of goods will be based on the principles of "the Harmonized Commodity Description and Coding System". Concerning imports referred to in Article VII of this Protocol (Agriculture), the provisions of that Article will apply.

3. For the purposes of para 2(a) above, the Palestinian market needs for 1994 will be estimated by a sub-committee of experts. These estimates will be based on the best available data regarding past consumption, production, investment and external trade of the Areas. The sub-committee will submit its estimate within three months from the signing of the Agreement. These estimates will be reviewed and updated every six months by the sub-committee, on the basis of the best data available regarding the latest period for which relevant data are available, taking into consideration all relevant economic and social indicators. Pending an agreement on the Palestinian market needs, the previous period's estimates adjusted for population growth and rise in per-capita GNP in the previous period, will serve as provisional estimates.

4. The Palestinian Authority will have all powers and responsibilities to independently determine and change from time to time the rates of customs, purchase taxes; levies, excises and other charges on the goods on List B, attached hereto as Appendix III, of basic food items and other goods for the Palestinian economic development program, imported by the Palestinians to the Areas.

5. a. With respect to all goods not specified in Lists A1, A2 and B, and with respect to quantities exceeding those determined in accordance with paras 2(a) & 3 above (hereinafter – the Quantities), the Israeli rates of customs, purchase tax, levies, excises and other charges, prevailing at the date of signing of the Agreement, as changed from time to time, shall serve as the minimum basis for the Palestinian Authority. The Palestinian Authority may decide on any upward changes in the rates on these goods and exceeding quantities when imported by the Palestinians to the Areas.

b. With respect to all goods not specified in Lists A1 and A2, and with respect to quantities exceeding the Quantities, Israel and the Palestinian Authority will employ for all imports the same system of importation, as stipulated in para 10 below, including inter alia standards, licensing, country of origin, valuation for customs purposes etc.

6. Each side will notify the other side immediately of changes made in rates and in other matters of import policy, regulations and procedures, determined by it within its respective powers and responsibilities as detailed in this Article. With regard to changes which do not require immediate application upon decision, there will be a process of advance notifications and mutual consultations which will take into consideration all aspects and economic implications.

7. The Palestinian Authority will levy VAT at one rate on both locally produced goods and services and on imports by the Palestinians (whether covered by the three Lists mentioned above or not), and may fix it at the level of 15% to 16%.

8. Goods imported from Jordan, Egypt and other Arab countries according to para 2(a)(1) above (List A1) will comply with rules of origin agreed upon by a joint sub-committee within three months of the date of the signing of the Agreement. Pending an agreement, goods will be considered to have been "locally produced" in any of those countries if they conform with all the following:

a. (i) They have been wholly grown, produced, or manufactured in that country, or have been substantially transformed there into new or different goods, having a new name, character, or use, distinct from the goods or materials from which they were so transformed;

(ii) They have been imported directly from the said country;

(iii) The value or the costs of the materials produced in that country, plus the direct processing costs in it, do not fall short of 30 percent of the export value of the goods. This rate may be reviewed by the joint committee mentioned in para 16 a year after the signing of the Agreement.

(iv) The goods are accompanied by an internationally recognized certificate of origin;

(v) No goods will be deemed as substantially new or different goods, and no material will be eligible for inclusion as domestic content, by virtue of having merely undergone simple combining or packaging, or dilution with water or other substances, which do not materially alter the characteristics of the said goods.

9. Each side will issue import licences to its own importers, subject to the principles of this Article and will be responsible for the implementation of the licensing requirements and procedures prevailing at the time of the issuance of the licenses.

Mutual arrangements will be made for the exchange of information relevant to licensing matters.

10. Except for the goods on Lists A1 and A2 and their Quantities – in which the Palestinian Authority has all powers and responsibilities – both sides will maintain the same import policy (except for rates of import taxes and other charges for goods in List B) and regulations including classification, valuation and other customs procedures, which are based

on the principles governing international codes, and the same policies of import licensing and of standards for imported goods, all as applied by Israel with respect to its importation. Israel may from time to time introduce changes in any of the above, provided that changes in standard requirements will not constitute a non-tariff-barrier and will be based on considerations of health, safety and the protection of the environment in conformity with Article 2.2. of the Agreement on Technical Barriers to trade of the Final Act of the Uruguay Round of Trade Negotiations.

Israel will give the Palestinian Authority prior notice of any such changes, and the provisions of para 6 above will apply.

11. a. The Palestinian Authority will determine its own rates of customs and purchase tax on motor vehicles imported as such, to be registered with the Palestinian Authority. The vehicle standards will be those applied at the date of the signing of the Agreement as changed according to para 10 above.

However, the Palestinian Authority may request, through the sub-committee on transportation, that in special cases different standards will apply.

Used motor vehicles will be imported only if they are passenger cars or dual-purpose passenger cars of a model of no more than three years prior to the importation year. The sub-committee on transportation will determine the procedures for testing and confirming that such used cars comply with the standards' requirements for that model year.

The issue of importing commercial vehicles of a model prior to the importation year will be discussed in the joint sub-committee mentioned in para 16 below.

b. Each side may determine the terms and conditions for the transfer of motor vehicles registered in the other side to the ownership or use of a resident of its own side, including the payment of the difference of import taxes, if any, and the vehicle having been tested and found compatible with the standards required at that time by its own registration administration, and may prohibit transfer of vehicles.

12. a. Jordanian standards, as specified in the attached Appendix I, will be acceptable in importing petroleum products into the Areas, once they meet the average of the standards existing in the European Union countries, or the USA standards, which parameters have been set at the values prescribed for the geographical conditions of Israel, the Gaza Strip and the West Bank.

Cases of petroleum products which do not meet these specifications will be referred to a joint experts' committee for a suitable solution. The committee may mutually decide to accept different standards for the importation of gasoline which meet the Jordanian standards even though, in some of their parameters, they do not meet the European Community or USA standards. The committee will give its decision within six months.

Pending the committee's decision, and for not longer than six months of the signing of the Agreement, the Palestinian Authority may import to the Areas, gasoline for the Palestinian market in the Areas, according to the needs of this market, provided that:

  (1) this gasoline is marked in a distinctive colour to differentiate it from the gasoline marketed in Israel; and

  (2) the Palestinian Authority will take all the necessary steps to ensure that this gasoline is not marketed in Israel.

  b. The difference in the final price of gasoline to consumers in Israel and to consumers in the Areas, will not exceed 15% of the official final consumer price in Israel. The Palestinian Authority has the right to determine the prices of petroleum products, other than gasoline, for consumption in the Areas.

  c. If Egyptian gasoline standards will comply with the conditions of sub-para (a) above, the importation of Egyptian gasoline will also be allowed.

13. In addition to the points of exit and entry designated according to the Article regarding Passages in Annex I of the Agreement for the purpose of export and import of goods, the Palestinian side has the right to use all points of exit and entry in Israel designated for that purpose. The import and export of the Palestinians through the points of exit and entry in Israel will be given equal trade and economic treatment.

14. In the entry points of the Jordan River and the Gaza Strip:

  a. Freight shipment. The Palestinian Authority will have full responsibility and powers in the Palestinian customs points (freight-area) for the implementation of the agreed upon customs and importation policy as specified in this protocol, including the inspection and the collection of taxes and other charges, when due.

  Israeli customs officials will be present and will receive from the Palestinian customs officials a copy of the necessary relevant documents related to the specific shipment and will be entitled to ask for inspection in their presence of both goods and tax collection.

  The Palestinian customs officials will be responsible for the handling of the customs procedure including the inspection and collection of due taxes.

  In case of disagreement on the clearance of any shipment according to this Article, the shipment will be delayed for inspection for a maximum period of 48 hours during which a joint sub-committee will resolve the issue on the basis of the relevant provisions of this Article. The shipment will be released only upon the sub-committee's decision.

b. Passengers customs lane. Each side will administer its own passengers customs procedures, including inspection and tax collection. The inspection and collection of taxes due in the Palestinian customs lane will be conducted by customs officials of the Palestinian Authority. Israeli customs officials will be invisibly present in the Palestinian customs lane and entitled to request inspection of goods and collection of taxes when due. In the case of suspicion, the inspection will be carried out by the Palestinian official in a separate room in the presence of the Israeli customs official.

15. The clearance of revenues from all import taxes and levies, between Israel and the Palestinian Authority, will be based on the principle of the place of final destination. In addition, these tax revenues will be allocated to the Palestinian Authority even if the importation was carried out by Israeli importers when the final destination explicitly stated in the import documentation is a corporation registered by the Palestinian Authority and conducting business activity in the Areas. This revenue clearance will be effected within six working days from the day of collection of the said taxes and levies.

16. The Joint Economic Committee or a sub-committee established by it for the purposes of this Article will deal inter alia with the following:

(1) Palestinian proposals for addition of items to Lists A1, A2 and B. Proposals for changes in rates and in import procedures, classification, standards and licensing requirements for all other imports;

(2) Estimate the Palestinian market needs, as mentioned in para 3 above;

(3) Receive notifications of changes and conduct consultations, as mentioned in para 6 above;

(4) Agree upon the rules of origin as mentioned in para 8 above, and review their implementation;

(5) Co-ordinate the exchange of information relevant to licensing matters as mentioned in para 9 above.

(6) Discuss and review any other matters concerning the implementation of this Article and resolve problems arising therefrom.

17. The Palestinian Authority will have the right to exempt the Palestinian returnees who will be granted permanent residency in the Areas from import taxes on personal belongings including house appliances and passenger cars as long as they are for personal use.

18. The Palestinian Authority will develop its system for temporary entry of needed machines and vehicles used for the Palestinian Authority and the Palestinian economic development plan.

Concerning other machines and equipment, not included in Lists A1, A2 and B, the temporary entry will be part of the import policy as agreed in para 10 above, until the joint sub-committee mentioned in para 16 decides upon a new system proposed by the Palestinian Authority. The temporary entry will be coordinated through the joint sub-committee.

19. Donations in kind to the Palestinian Authority will be exempted from customs and other import taxes if destined and used for defined development projects or non-commercial humanitarian purposes.

The Palestinian Authority will be responsible exclusively for planning and management of the donors' assistance to the Palestinian people. The Joint Economic Committee will discuss issues pertaining to the relations between the provisions in this Article and the implementation of the principles in the above paragraph.

Article IV
MONETARY AND FINANCIAL ISSUES
1. The Palestinian Authority will establish a Monetary Authority (PMA) in the Areas.

The PMA will have the powers and responsibilities for the regulation and implementation of the monetary policies within the functions described in this Article.
2. The PMA will act as the Palestinian Authority's official economic and financial advisor.
3. The PMA will act as the Palestinian Authority's and the public sector entities' sole financial agent, locally and internationally.
4. The foreign currency reserves (including gold) of the Palestinian Authority and all Palestinian public sector entities will be deposited solely with the PMA and managed by it.
5. The PMA will act as the lender of last resort for the banking system in the Areas.
6. The PMA will authorize foreign exchange dealers in the Areas and will exercise control (regulation and supervision) over foreign exchange transactions within the Areas and with the rest of the world.
7. a. The PMA will have a banking supervision department that will be responsible for the proper functioning, stability, solvency and liquidity of the banks operating in the Areas.
   b. The banking supervision department will predicate its supervision on the international principles and standards reflected in international conventions and especially on the principles of the "Basle Committee".
   c. The supervision department will be charged with the general supervision of every such bank, including:
   – The regulation of all kinds of banking activities, including their foreign activities;
   – The licensing of banks formed locally and of branches, subsidiaries, joint ventures and representative offices of foreign banks and the approval of controlling shareholders;
   – The supervision and inspection of banks.
8. The PMA will relicense each of the five branches of the Israeli banks operating at present in the Gaza Strip and the West Bank, as soon as its

location or the authorities regarding it come under the jurisdiction of the Palestinian Authority. These branches will be required to comply with the general rules and regulations of the PMA concerning foreign banks, based on the "Basle Concordat". Para 10 d, e, and f below will apply to these branches.

9.   a. Any other Israeli bank wishing to open a branch or a subsidiary in the Areas will apply for a license to the PMA and will be treated equally to other foreign banks, provided that the same will apply to the Palestinian banks wishing to open a branch or a subsidiary in Israel.

b. Granting of a license by both authorities will be subject to the following arrangements based on the "Basle Concordat" valid on the date of signing of the Agreement and to the host authority's prevailing general rules and regulations concerning opening of branches and subsidiaries of foreign banks.

In this para 10 "host authority" and "home authority" apply only to the Bank of Israel (BOI) and the PMA.

c. A bank wishing to open a branch or establish a subsidiary will apply to the host authority, having first obtained the approval of its home authority. The host authority will notify the home authority of the terms of the license, and will give its final approval unless the home authority objects.

d. The home authority will be responsible for the consolidated and comprehensive supervision of banks, inclusive of branches and subsidiaries in the area under the jurisdiction of the host authority. However, the distribution of supervision responsibilities between the home and the host authorities concerning subsidiaries will be according to the "Basle Concordat".

e. The host authority will regularly examine the activities of branches and subsidiaries in the area under its jurisdiction.

The home authority will have the right to conduct on site examinations in the branches and subsidiaries in the host area. However, the supervision responsibilities of the home authority concerning subsidiaries will be according to the "Basle Concordat".

Accordingly, each authority will transfer to the other authority copies of its examination reports and any information relevant to the solvency, stability and soundness of the banks, their branches and subsidiaries.

f. The BOI and the PMA will establish a mechanism for cooperation and for the exchange of information on issues of mutual interest.

10.   a. The New Israeli Sheqel (NIS) will be one of the circulating currencies in the Areas and will legally serve there as means of payment for all purposes including official transactions.

Any circulating currency, including the NIS, will be accepted by the Palestinian Authority and by all its institutions, local authorities and banks, when offered as a means of payment for any transaction.

b. Both sides will continue to discuss, through the JEC, the possibility of introducing mutually agreed Palestinian currency or temporary alternative currency arrangements for the Palestinian Authority.

11. a. The liquidity requirements on all deposits in banks operating in the Areas will be determined and announced by the PMA.

b. Banks in the Areas will accept NIS deposits. The liquidity requirements on the various kinds of NIS deposits (or deposits linked to the NIS) in banks operating in the Areas will not be less than 4% to 8%, according to the type of deposits. Changes of over 1% in the liquidity requirements on NIS deposits (or deposits linked to the NIS) in Israel will call for corresponding changes in the above mentioned rates.

c. The supervision and inspection of the implementation of all liquidity requirements will be carried out by the PMA.

d. The reserves and the liquid assets required according to this paragraph will be deposited at the PMA according to rules and regulations determined by it. Penalties for non compliance with the liquidity requirements will be determined by the PMA.

12. The PMA will regulate and administer a discount window system and the supply of temporary finance for banks operating in the Areas.

13. a. The PMA will establish or license a clearing house in order to clear money orders between the banks operating in the Areas, and with other clearing houses.

b. The clearing of money orders and transactions between banks operating in the Areas and banks operating in Israel will be done between the Israeli and the Palestinian clearing houses on same working day basis, according to agreed arrangements.

14. Both sides will allow correspondential relations between each others' banks.

15. The PMA will have the right to convert at the BOI excess NIS received from banks operating in the Areas into foreign currency, in which the BOI trades in the domestic inter-bank market, up to the amounts determined per period, according to the arrangements detailed in para 16 below.

16. a. The excess amount of NIS, due to balance of payments flows, that the PMA will have the right to convert into foreign currency, will be equal to:

(1) Estimates of all Israeli "imports" of goods and services from the Areas, valued at market prices (inclusive of taxes), which were paid for in NIS, less:

(i) the taxes collected by the Palestinian Authority on all Israeli "imports" from the Areas and rebated to Israel in NIS, and

(ii) the taxes collected by Israel on all Israeli "imports" from the Areas and included in their market value, and not rebated to the Palestinian Authority, minus

(2) Estimates of all Israeli "exports" of goods and services to the Areas, valued at market prices (inclusive of taxes), which were paid for in NIS, less:

(i) the taxes collected by Israel on such "exports" and rebated to the Palestinian Authority, and

(ii) the taxes collected by the Palestinian Authority on such "exports" and included in their market value, and not rebated to Israel; plus

(3) The accumulated net amounts of foreign currency converted previously into NIS by the PMA, as recorded in the BOI Dealing Room.

b. The said flows and amounts will be calculated as of the date of the signing of the Agreement

Notes to para 16:

(i) The estimates of the said "exports and imports" of goods and services will include inter alia labor services, NIS expenditure of tourists and Israelis in the Areas and NIS expenditure of Palestinians of the Areas in Israel.

(ii) Taxes and pension contributions on "imports" of labor services, paid to "importing" side and rebated to the "exporting" one, will not be included in the estimates of the sums to be converted, as the "exports'" earnings of labor services are recorded in the statistics inclusive of them, although they do not accrue to the individuals supplying them.

17. The PMA and the BOI will meet annually to discuss and determine the annual amount of convertible NIS during the following calendar year and will meet semi-annually to adjust the said amount. The amounts determined annually and adjusted semi-annually will be based on data and estimates regarding the past and on forecasts for the following period, according to the formula mentioned in para 16. The first meeting will be as soon as possible within three months after the date of the signing of the Agreement.

18. a. The exchange of foreign currency for NIS and vice-versa by the PMA will be carried out through the BOI Dealing Room, at the market exchange rates.

b. The BOI will not be obliged to convert in any single month more than $^1/_5$ of the semi-annual amount, as mentioned in para 17.

19. There will be no ceiling on the annual foreign currency conversions by the PMA into NIS. However, in order to avoid undesirable fluctuations in the foreign exchange market, monthly ceilings of such conversions will be agreed upon in the annual and semi-annual meetings referred to in para 17.

20. Banks in the Areas will convert NIS into other circulating currencies and vice-versa.

21. The Palestinian Authority will have the authorities, powers and responsibilities regarding the regulation and supervision of capital activities in the Areas, including the licensing of capital market institutions, finance companies and investment funds.

Article V
DIRECT TAXATION

1. Israel and the Palestinian Authority will each determine and regulate independently its own tax policy in matters of direct taxation, including income tax on individuals and corporations, property taxes, municipal taxes and fees.

2. Each tax administration will have the right to levy the direct taxes generated by economic activities within its area.

3. Each tax administration may impose additional taxes on residents within its area on [individuals and corporations] who conduct economic activities in the other side's area.

4. Israel will transfer to the Palestinian Authority a sum equal to:

   a. 75% of the income taxes collected from Palestinians from the Gaza Strip and the Jericho Area employed in Israel.

   b. The full amount of income taxes collected from Palestinians from the Gaza Strip and Jericho Area employed in the settlements.

5. The two sides will agree on a set of procedures that will address all issues concerning double taxation.

Article VI
INDIRECT TAXES ON LOCAL PRODUCTION

1. The Israel and the Palestinian tax administrations will levy and collect VAT and purchase taxes on local production, as well as any other indirect taxes, in their respective areas.

2. The purchase tax rates within the jurisdiction of each tax administration will be identical as regards locally produced and imported goods.

3. The present Israeli VAT rate is 17%. The Palestinian VAT rate will be 15% to 16%.

4. The Palestinian Authority will decide on the maximum annual turnover for businesses under its jurisdiction to be exempt from VAT, within an upper limit of 12,000 US $.

5. The VAT on purchases by businesses registered for VAT purposes will accrue to the tax administration with which the respective business is registered.

Businesses will register for VAT purposes with the tax administration of the side of their residence, or on the side of their ongoing operation.

There will be clearance of VAT revenues between the Israeli and Palestinian VAT administrations on the following conditions:

a. The VAT clearance will apply to VAT on transactions between businesses registered with the VAT administration of the side in which they reside.

b. The following procedures will apply to clearance of VAT revenues accruing from transactions by businesses registered for VAT purposes:

(1) To be acceptable for clearance purposes, special invoices, clearly marked for this purpose, will be used for transactions between businesses registered with the different sides.

(2) The invoices will be worded either in both Hebrew and Arabic or in English and will be filled out in any of these three languages, provided that the figures are written in "Arabic" (not Hindi) numerals.

(3) For the purpose of tax rebates, such invoices will be valid for six months from their date of issue.

(4) Representatives of the two sides will meet once a month, on the 20th day of the month, to present each other with a list of invoices submitted to them for tax rebate, for VAT clearance. This list will include the following details regarding each invoice:

(a) The number of the registered business issuing it;

(b) The name of the registered business issuing it;

(c) The number of the invoice;

(d) The date of issue;

(e) The amount of the invoice;

(f) The name of the recipient of the invoice.

(5) The clearance claims will be settled within 6 days from the meeting, through a payment by the side with the net balance of claims against it, to the other side.

(6) Each side will provide the other side, upon demand, with invoices for verification purposes. Each tax administration will be responsible for providing invoices for verification purposes for 6 months after receiving them.

(7) Each side will take the necessary measure to verify the authenticity of the invoices presented to it for clearance by the other side.

(8) Claims for VAT clearance which will not be found valid will be deducted from the next clearance payment.

(9) Once an inter-connected computer system for tax rebates to businesses and for VAT clearance between the two sides is operational, it will replace the clearance procedures specified in sub-paras (4)–(8).

(10) The two tax administrations will exchange lists of the businesses registered with them and will provide each other with the necessary documentation, if required, for the verification of transactions.

(11) The two sides will establish a sub-committee which will deal with the implementation arrangements regarding the clearance of VAT revenues set above.

6. VAT paid by not-for-profit Palestinian organizations and institutions, registered by the Palestinian Authority, on transactions in Israel, will accrue to the Palestinian tax administration. The clearance system set out in para 5 will apply to these organizations and institutions.

Article VII
LABOR
1. Both sides will attempt to maintain the normality of movement of labor between them, subject to each side's right to determine from time to time the extent and conditions of the labor movement into its area. If the normal movement is suspended temporarily by either side, it will give the other side immediate notification, and the other side may request that the matter be discussed in the Joint Economic Committee.

The placement and employment of workers from one side in the area of the other side will be through the employment service of the other side and in accordance with the other side's legislation.

The Palestinian side has the right to regulate the employment of Palestinian labor in Israel through the Palestinian employment service, and the Israeli Employment Service will cooperate and coordinate in this regard.

2.   a. Palestinians employed in Israel will be insured in the Israeli social insurance system according to the National Insurance Law for employment injuries that occur in Israel, bankruptcy of employers and maternity leave allowance.

b. The National Insurance fees deducted from the wages for maternity insurance will be reduced according to the reduced scope of maternity insurance, and the equalization deductions transferred to the Palestinian Authority, if levied, will be increased accordingly.

c. Implementation procedures relating thereto will be agreed upon between the Israeli National Insurance Institute and the Palestinian Authority or the appropriate Palestinian social insurance institution.

3.   a. Israel will transfer to the Palestinian Authority, on a monthly basis, the equalization deductions as defined by Israeli legislation, if imposed and to the extent levied by Israel. The sums so transferred will be used for social benefits and health services, decided upon by the Palestinian Authority, for Palestinians employed in Israel and for their families.

The equalization deductions to be so transferred will be those collected after the date of the signing of the Agreement from wages of Palestinians employed in Israel and from their employers.

These sums will not include

(1) Payments for health services in places of employment.

(2) $2/3$ of the actual administrative costs in handling the matters related to the Palestinians employed in Israel by the Payments Section of the Israeli Employment Service.

4. Israel will transfer, on a monthly basis, to a relevant pension insurance institution to be established by the Palestinian Authority, pension insurance deductions collected after the establishment of the above institution and the completion of the documents mentioned in para 6.

These deductions will be collected from wages of Palestinians employed in Israel and their employers, according to the relevant rates set out in the applicable Israeli collective agreements. $^2/_3$ of the actual administrative costs in handling these deductions by the Israeli Employment Service will be deducted from the sums transferred. The sums so transferred will be used for providing pension insurance for these workers. Israel will continue to be liable for pension rights of the Palestinian employees in Israel, to the extent accumulated by Israel before the entry into force of this para 4.

5. Upon the receipt of the deductions, the Palestinian Authority and its relevant social institutions will assume full responsibility in accordance with the Palestinian legislation and arrangements, for pension rights and other social benefits of Palestinians employed in Israel, that accrue from the transferred deductions related to these rights and benefits. Consequently, Israel and its relevant social institutions and the Israeli employers will be released from, and will not be held liable for any obligations and responsibilities concerning personal claims, rights and benefits arising from these transferred deductions, or from the provisions of paras 2–4 above.

6. Prior to the said transfers, the Palestinian Authority or its relevant institutions, as the case may be, will provide Israel with the documents required to give legal effect to their aforesaid obligations, including mutually agreed implementation procedures of the principles agreed upon in paras 3–5 above.

7. The above arrangements concerning equalization deductions and/or pension deductions may be reviewed and changed by Israel if an authorized court in Israel will determine that the deductions or any part thereof must be paid to individuals, or used for individual social benefits or insurance in Israel, or that it is otherwise unlawful. In such a case the liability of the Palestinian side will not exceed the actual transferred deductions related to the case.

8. Israel will respect any agreement reached between the Palestinian Authority, or an organization or trade-union representing the Palestinians employed in Israel, and a representative organization of employees or employers in Israel, concerning contributions to such organization according to any collective agreement.

9.   a. The Palestinian Authority may integrate the existing health insurance scheme for Palestinians employed in Israel and their families in its health insurance services. As long as this scheme continues, whether integrated or separately, Israel will deduct from

their wages the health insurance fees ("health stamp") and will transfer them to the Palestinian Authority for this purpose.

b. The Palestinian Authority may integrate the existing health insurance scheme for Palestinians who were employed in Israel and are receiving pension payments through the Israeli Employment Service, in its health insurance services. As long as this scheme continues, whether integrated or separately, Israel will deduct the necessary sum of health insurance fees ("health stamp") from the equalization payments and will transfer them to the Palestinian Authority for this purpose.

10. The JEC will meet upon the request of either side and review the implementation of this Article and other issues concerning labor, social insurance and social rights.

11. Other deductions not mentioned above, if any, will be jointly reviewed by the JEC. Any agreement between the two sides concerning these deductions will be in addition to the above provisions.

12. Palestinians employed in Israel will have the right to bring disputes arising out of employee–employer relationships and other issues before the Israeli Labor Courts, within these courts' jurisdiction.

13. This Article governs the future labor relations between the two sides and will not impair any labor rights prior to the date of signing of the Agreement.

Article VIII
AGRICULTURE

1. There will be free movement of agricultural produce, free of customs and import taxes, between the two sides, subject to the following exceptions and arrangements.

2. The official veterinary and plant protection services of each side will be responsible, within the limits of their respective jurisdiction, for controlling animal health, animal products and biological products, and plants and parts thereof, as well as their importation and exportation.

3. The relations between the official veterinary and plant protection services of both sides will be based on mutuality in accordance with the following principles, which will be applied in all the areas under their respective jurisdiction:

a. Israel and the Palestinian Authority will do their utmost to preserve and improve the veterinary standards.

b. Israel and the Palestinian Authority will take all measures to reach equivalent and compatible standards regarding animal disease control, including mass vaccination of animals and avians, quarantines, "stamping out" measures and residue control standards.

c. Mutual arrangements will be made to prevent the introduction and spread of plant pests and diseases, for their eradication and concerning residue control standards in plant products.

d. The official veterinary and plant protection services of Israel and the Palestinian Authority will co-ordinate and regularly exchange information regarding animal diseases, as well as plant pests and diseases, and will establish a mechanism for immediate notification of the outbreak of such diseases.

4. Trade between the two sides in animals, animal products and biological products will be in keeping with the principles and definitions set out in the current edition of the OIE National Animal Health Code as updated from time to time (hereinafter – I.A.H.C.)

5. Transit of livestock, animal products and biological products from one side through the area under the jurisdiction of the other side, should be conducted in a manner aimed at the prevention of diseases spreading to or from the consignment during its movement. For such a transit to be permitted, it is a prerequisite that the veterinary conditions agreed upon by both sides will be met in regard to importation of animals, their products and biological products from external markets. Therefore the parties agree to the following arrangements.

6. The official veterinary services of each side have the authority to issue veterinary import permits for import of animals, animal products and biological products to the areas under its jurisdiction. In order to prevent the introduction of animal diseases from third parties, the following procedures will be adopted:

a. The import permits will strictly follow the professional veterinary conditions for similar imports to Israel as prevailing at the time of their issuance. The permits will specify the country of origin and the required conditions to be included in the official veterinary certificates which should be issued by the veterinary authorities in the countries of origin and which should accompany each consignment.

Each side may propose a change in these conditions. The change will come into force 10 days after notice to the other side, unless the other side requested that the matter be brought before the Veterinary Sub-Committee specified in para 14 (hereinafter – VSC). If it is more stringent than the prevailing conditions – it will come into force 20 days after the request, unless both sides decide otherwise through the VSC, and if more lenient – it will come into force only if agreed upon by both sides through the VSC.

However, if the change is urgent and needed for the protection of animal and public health, it will come into force immediately after notice by the other side and will remain in force unless and until both sides agree otherwise through the VSC.

b. The official veterinary certificates will include the provisions regarding OIE Lists A & B Diseases as specified in the I.A.H.C. When the I.A.H.C. allows alternative requirements regarding the same disease, the most stringent one will be adopted unless otherwise agreed upon by the VSC.

c. When infectious diseases which are not included in Lists A & B of the I.A.H.C. exist or are suspected, on scientific grounds, to exist in the exporting country, the necessary veterinary import conditions that will be required and included in the official veterinary certificates, will be discussed in the VSC, and in the case of different professional opinions, the most stringent ones will be adopted.

d. The import of live vaccines will be permitted only if so decided by the VSC.

e. Both sides will exchange, through the VSC, information pertaining to import licensing, including the evaluation of the disease situation and zoosanitary capability of exporting countries, which will be based upon official information as well as upon other available data.

f. Consignments which do not conform with the above mentioned requirements will not be permitted to enter the areas under the jurisdiction of either side.

7. Transportation of livestock and poultry and of animal products and biological products between areas under the jurisdiction of one side through areas under the jurisdiction of the other side, will be subject to the following technical rules: a. The transportation will be by vehicles which will be sealed with a seal of the official veterinary services of the place of origin and marked with a visible sign "Animal Transportation" or "Products of Animal Origin" in Arabic and Hebrew, in coloured and clearly visible letters on white background.; b. Each consignment will be accompanied by a veterinary certificate issued by the official veterinary services of the place of origin, certifying that the animals or their products were examined and are free of infectious diseases and originate from a place which is not under quarantine or under animal movement restrictions.

8. Transportation of livestock and poultry, animal products and biological products destined for Israel from the Areas and vice versa will be subject to veterinary permits issued by the official veterinary services of the recipient side, in keeping with the OIE standards used in international traffic in this field. Each such consignment will be transported by a suitable and marked vehicle, accompanied by a veterinary certificate in the form agreed upon between the official veterinary services of both sides. Such certificates will be issued only if permits of the recipient side are presented.

9. In order to prevent the introduction of plant pests and diseases to the region, the following procedures will be adopted :

a. The transportation between the Areas and Israel, of plants and parts thereof (including fruits and vegetables), the control of pesticide residues in them and the transportation of plant propagation material and of animal feed, may be inspected without delay or damage by the plant protection services of the recipient side.

b. The transportation between the Areas through Israel of plants and parts thereof (including fruits and vegetables) as well as of pesticides, may be required to pass a phytosanitary inspection without delay or damage.

c. The official Palestinian plant protection services have the authority to issue permits for the import of plants and parts thereof as well as of pesticides from external markets. The permits will be based on the prevailing standards and requirements.

The permits will specify the required conditions to be included in the official Phytosanitary Certificates (hence P.C.) based upon the standards and the requirements of the International Plant Protection Convention (I.P.P.C.) and those of the European and Mediterranean Plant Protection Organization (E.P.P.O.) which should accompany each consignment.

The P.C.'s will be issued by the plant protection services in the countries of origin. Dubious or controversial cases will be brought before the sub-committee on plant protection.

10. The agricultural produce of both sides will have free and unrestricted access to each others' markets, with the temporary exception of sales from one side to the other side of the following items only: poultry, eggs, potatoes, cucumbers, tomatoes and melons. The temporary restrictions on these items will be gradually removed on an increasing scale until they are finally eliminated by 1998, as listed below: [Table showing quantities ommitted. In 1994, poultry exports are set at 5,000 tons, eggs at 30 million, potatoes at 10,000 tons, cucumbers at 10,000 tons, tomatoes at 13,000 tons and melons at 10,000 tons. For 1995 these figures increase to 6,000 tons of poultry, 40 million eggs, 13,000 tons of potatoes, 13,000 tons of cucumbers, 16,000 tons of tomatoes and 13,000 tons of melons. The amounts increase until 1998, after which exports are unlimited]. The Palestinian Authority will notify Israel the apportioning of these quantities between these areas concerning the quantities pertaining to the Palestinian produce.

11. The Palestinians will have the right to export their agricultural produce to external markets without restrictions, on the basis of certificates of origin issued by the Palestinian Authority.

12. Without prejudice to obligations arising out of existing international agreements, the two sides will refrain from importing agricultural products from third parties which may adversely affect the interests of each other's farmers.

13. Each side will take the necessary measures in the area under its jurisdiction to prevent damage which may be caused by its agriculture to the environment of the other side.

14. The two sides will establish sub-committees of their respective official veterinary and plant protection services, which will update the information

and review issues, policies and procedures in these fields. Any changes in the provisions of this Article will be agreed upon by both sides.

15. The two sides will establish a sub-committee of experts in the dairy sector in order to exchange information, discuss and coordinate their production in this sector so as to protect the interests of both sides. In principle, each side will produce according to its domestic consumption.

Article IX
INDUSTRY

1. There will be free movement of industrial goods free of any restrictions including customs and import taxes between the two sides, subject to each side's legislation.
2.   a. The Palestinian side has the right to employ various methods in encouraging and promoting the development of the Palestinian industry by way of providing grants, loans, research and development assistance and direct-tax benefits.
   The Palestinian side has also the right to employ other methods of encouraging industry resorted to in Israel.
   b. Both sides will exchange information about the methods employed by them in the encouragement of their respective industries.
   c. Indirect tax rebates or benefits and other subsidies to sales shall not be allowed in trade between the two sides.
3. Each side will do its best to avoid damage to the industry of the other side and will take into consideration the concerns of the other side in its industrial policy.
4. Both sides will cooperate in the prevention of deceptive practices, trade in goods which may endanger health, safety and the environment and in goods of expired validity.
5. Each side will take the necessary measures in the area under its jurisdiction to prevent damage which may be caused by its industry to the environment of the other side.
6. The Palestinians will have the right to export their industrial produce to external markets without restrictions, on the basis of certificates of origin issued by the Palestinian Authority.
7. The JEC will meet and review issues pertaining to this Article.

Article X
TOURISM

1. The Palestinian Authority will establish a Palestinian Tourism Authority which will exercise, inter alia, the following powers in the Areas.
   a. Regulating, licensing, classifying and supervising tourist services, sites and industries.
   b. Promoting foreign and domestic tourism and developing the Palestinian tourist resources and sites.

c. Supervising the marketing, promotion and information activities related to foreign and domestic tourism.

2. Each side shall, under its respective jurisdiction, protect, guard and ensure the maintenance and good upkeep of historical, archaeological, cultural and religious sites and all other tourist sites, to fit their status as well as their purpose as a destination for visitors.

3. Each side will determine reasonable visiting hours and days for all tourist sites in order to facilitate visits at a wide variety of days and hours, taking into consideration religious and national holidays. Each side shall publicize such opening times.

Meaningful changes in the opening times will take into consideration tourist programs already committed to.

4. Tourist buses or any other form of tourist transport authorized by either side, and operated by companies registered and licensed by it, will be allowed to enter and proceed on their tour within the area under the jurisdiction of the other side, provided that such buses or other vehicles conform with the EEC technical specifications [I. currently adopted]. All such vehicles will be clearly marked as tourist vehicles.

5. Each side will protect the environment and the ecology around the tourist sites under its jurisdiction. In view of the importance of beaches and maritime activities for tourism, each side will do its best efforts to ensure that development and construction on the Mediterranean coast, and especially at ports (such as Ashqelon or Gaza), will be planned and carried out in a manner that will not adversely affect the ecology, environment or the functions of the coastline and beaches of the other side.

6. Tourism companies and agencies licensed by either side shall enjoy equal access to tourism – related facilities and amenities in border points of exit and entry according to the regulations of the authority operating them.

7. a. Each side will license, according to its own rules and regulations, travel agents, tour companies, tour guides and other tourism businesses (hereinafter – tourism entities) within its jurisdiction.

b. Tourism entities authorized by either side, will be allowed to conduct tours that include the area under the jurisdiction of the other side, provided that their authorization as well as their operation will be in accordance with rules, professional requirements and standards agreed upon by both sides in the sub-committee mentioned in para 9.

Pending that agreement, existing tourism entities in the Areas which are currently allowed to conduct tours that include Israel, will be allowed to continue to do so, and Israeli authorized tourism entities will continue to be allowed to conduct tours that include the Areas. In addition, any tourism entity of one side that the tourism authorities of the other side will certify as fulfilling all its rules, professional requirements and standards, will be allowed to conduct tours that include that other side.

8. Each side will make its own arrangement for compensation of tourists for bodily injury and property damages caused by political violence in the areas under its respective jurisdiction.

9. The JEC or a tourism sub-committee established by it shall meet upon the request of either side in order to discuss the implementation of the provisions of this Article and resolve problems that may arise. The sub-committee will also discuss and consider tourist issues of benefit to both sides, and will promote educational programs for tourism entities of both sides in order to further their professional standards and their ethics. Complaints of one side against the behaviour of tourism entities of the other side will be channelled through the committee.

Note: It is agreed that the final wording in the last sentence in para 4 will be adopted according to the final wording in the relevant provisions of the Agreement.

Article XI
INSURANCE ISSUES

1. The authorities, powers and responsibilities in the insurance sphere in the Areas, including inter alia the licensing of insurers, insurance agents and the supervision of their activities, will be transferred to the Palestinian Authority.

2. a. The Palestinian Authority will maintain a compulsory absolute liability system for road accident victims with a ceiling on the amount of compensation based upon the following principles:

(1) Absolute liability for death or bodily injury to road accident victims, it being immaterial whether or not there was fault on the part of the driver and whether or not there was fault or contributory fault on the part of others, each driver being responsible for persons travelling in his vehicle and for pedestrians hit by his vehicle.

(2) Compulsory insurance for all motor vehicles, covering death or bodily injury to all road accident victims, including drivers.

(3) No cause of action in tort for death or bodily injury resulting from road accidents.

(4) The maintenance of a statutory fund (hereinafter – the Fund) for compensation of road accident victims who are unable to claim compensation from an insurer for the following reasons:

(i) the driver liable for compensation is unknown;

(ii) the driver is not insured or his insurance does not cover the liability involved; or

(iii) the insurer is unable to meet his liabilities.

b. Terms in this Article will have the same meaning as in the legislation prevailing at the date of signing of the Agreement concerning compulsory motor vehicle insurance and compensation of road accident victims.

c. Any change by either side in the rules and regulations regarding the implementation of the above mentioned principles will require prior notice to the other side. A change which might substantially affect the other side will require prior notice of at least three months.

3.   a. Upon the signing of the Agreement the Palestinian Authority will establish a Fund for the Areas (hereinafter – the Palestinian Fund) for the purposes detailed in para 2(a)(4) above and for the purposes detailed below. The Palestinian Fund will assume the responsibilities of the statutory Road Accident Victims Compensation Fund in the West Bank and the Gaza Strip (hereinafter – the Existing Fund) regarding the Areas, according to the prevailing law at that time. Accordingly, the Existing Fund will cease to be responsible for any liability regarding accidents occurring in the Areas from the date of signing of the Agreement.

b. The Existing Fund will transfer to the Palestinian Fund, after the assumption of the above mentioned responsibilities by it, the premiums paid to the Existing Fund by the insurers for vehicles registered in the Areas, pro-rata to the unexpired period of each insurance policy.

4.   a. Compulsory motor vehicle insurance policies issued by insurers licensed by either side will be valid in the territories of both sides. Accordingly, a vehicle registered in one side covered by such a policy will not be required to have an additional insurance coverage for travel in the areas under the other side's jurisdiction. These insurance policies will cover all the liabilities according to the legislation of the place of the accident.

b. In order to cover part of the liabilities which may incur due to road accidents in Israel by uninsured vehicles registered in the Palestinian Authority, the Palestinian Fund will transfer to the Israeli Fund, on a monthly basis, for each insured vehicle, an amount equal to 30% of the amount paid to the Israeli Fund by an insurer registered in Israel, for the sat-ne type of vehicle, for the same period of insurance (which will not be less than 90 days).

5. In cases where a victim of a road accident wishes to claim compensation from an insurer registered by the other side or from the Fund of the other side or in cases where a driver or an owner of a car is sued by a victim, by an insurer or by the Fund of the other side, he may nominate the Fund of his side as his proxy for this purpose. The Fund so nominated may address any relevant party from the other side directly or through the other sides' Fund.

6. In the case of a road accident in which neither the registration number of the vehicle nor the identity of the driver are known, the Fund of the side which has jurisdiction over the place of the accident will compensate the victim, according to its own legislation.

7. The Fund of each side will be responsible towards the victims of the other side for any liability of the insurers of its side regarding the compulsory insurance and will guarantee their liabilities.

8. Each side will guarantee its Fund's liabilities according to this Article.

9. The two sides will negotiate within three months from the date of the signing of the Agreement a cut-off agreement between the Existing Fund and the Palestinian Fund concerning accidents which occurred in the Areas prior to the date of the signing of the Agreement, whether claims have been reported or not. The cut-off agreement will not include compensation for Israeli victims involved in accidents which occurred in the Areas prior to the date of the signing of the Agreement.

10. a. The two sides will establish immediately upon the signing of the Agreement, a sub-committee of experts (hereinafter – the Sub-Committee) which will deal with issues regarding the implementation of this Article, including:

(1) Procedures concerning the handling of claims of victims of the one side from insurers or from the Fund of the other side;

(2) Procedures concerning the transfer of the amounts between the Funds of both sides as mentioned in para 4(b) above;

(3) The details of the cut-off agreement between the Existing Fund and the Palestinian Fund, as set out in para 9 above;

(4) Any other relevant issue raised by either side.

b. The Sub-Committee will act as a continuous committee for issues regarding this Article.

c. The two sides will exchange, through the Sub-Committee, the relevant information regarding the implementation of this Article, including police reports, medical information, relevant statistics, premiums, etc. The two sides will provide each other with any other assistance required in this regard.

11. Each side may require the re-examination of the arrangements set out in this Article a year after the date of the signing of the Agreement.

12. Insurers from both sides may apply for a license to the relevant authorities of the other side, according to the rules and regulations regarding foreign insurers in the latter side. The two sides agree not to discriminate against such applicants.

Done in Paris, this twenty ninth day of April, 1994 For the Government of Israel. For the PLO. Finance Minister Avraham Shohat Abu Ala (Ahmed Korei).

Index

Note: Italic references are to the maps. Bold numbers refer to pages in the Appendices. The Appendices have been indexed only for subjects covered in the main text.

140